Prayers
for Schools

Original prayers and resources
for teachers and chaplains

RAYMOND FRIEL

Prayers
for Schools

Original prayers and resources for teachers and chaplains

redemptorist
publications

Published by Redemptorist Publications
Wolf's Lane, Chawton, Hampshire GU34 3HQ, UK
Tel. +44 (0)1420 88222. Fax +44 (0)1420 88805
Email rp@rpbooks.co.uk, www.rpbooks.co.uk

A registered charity limited by guarantee.
Registered in England 03261721

Copyright © Redemptorist Publications 2018
First published 2018
Second printing December 2019

Edited by Barbara Spender
Designed by Eliana Thompson

ISBN 978-0-85231-492-0

A CIP catalogue record for this book is available from the British Library.

The publisher gratefully acknowledges permission to use the following copyright material:

Excerpts from The Jerusalem Bible, copyright © 1966 by Darton, Longman & Todd, Ltd and Doubleday, a division of Random House, Inc. Reprinted by permission.

Printed and bound by Lithgo Press Ltd., Leicester LE8 6NU

ACKNOWLEDGEMENTS

I would like to thank all the school and college chaplains and teachers who sent me case studies from their schools, they are all named in Part III. I would like to thank in particular Clare Hogg, headteacher of St Thomas More School in Crewe and Julie-Anne Tallon, headteacher of Abbey Primary School in Birmingham, two outstanding faith leaders who welcomed me to their schools and allowed me to interview some of their wonderful pupils. Thank you to Sr Judith Russi, friend and co-conspirator, who was very generous with her time and resources built up over many years working in schools. Thanks to the team at Redemptorist Publications for their great support and hearty lunches, especially to Barbara Spender, my editor on this project. As ever, I'd like to thank my wife Janet for her love, patience and humour through the highs and lows of another book.

CONTENTS

DEDICATION

*To all our young people who come to the well with their "empty jars"
looking for refreshment and friendship, may we who are entrusted with their care
offer them the living water of the Gospel.*

BY THE SAME AUTHOR

Books/Journals

Seeing the River
(Edinburgh: Polygon, 1995)

Southfields Vol 1-6, ed. with Richard Price
(London: Southfields Press, 1995-2000)

Renfrewshire in Old Photographs, with Richard Price
(Glasgow: Mariscat, 2000)

PS Nos 1-7, ed. with Richard Price
(London: published by Richard Price, 2006-2012)

Stations of the Heart
(Cambridge: Salt, 2008)

How to Survive Working in a Catholic School, with Sister Judith Russi
(Chawton: Redemptorist Publications, 2013)

How to Survive in Leadership in a Catholic School
(Chawton: Redemptorist Publications, 2015)

The Revolution of Tenderness: Being a Catholic in Today's Church
(Chawton: Redemptorist Publications, 2016)

Gospel Values for Catholic Schools: a practical guide for today
(Chawton: Redemptorist Publications, 2017)

Audio/CD

The Hope that is Within You: Timothy Radcliffe in Conversation with Raymond Friel, CD and Transcript (Chawton: Redemptorist Publications, 2016)

The Hope that is Within You: Gemma Simmonds in Conversation with Raymond Friel, CD and Transcript (Chawton: Redemptorist Publications, 2017)

The Hope that is Within You: Eamon Duffy in Conversation with Raymond Friel, CD and Transcript (Chawton: Redemptorist Publications, 2017)

The Hope that is Within You: Judith Russi in Conversation with Raymond Friel, CD and Transcript (Chawton: Redemptorist Publications, 2017)

The Hope that is Within You: Padraig O'Tuama in Conversation with Raymond Friel, CD and Transcript (Chawton: Redemptorist Publications, 2017)

The Hope that is Within You: Jean Vanier in Conversation with Raymond Friel, CD and Transcript (Chawton: Redemptorist Publications, 2018)

"Now it happened in those days that he went onto the mountain to pray;
and he spent the whole night in prayer to God."

(Luke 6:12)

Jesus Christ's repeated recourse to prayer prior to the most significant moments of his public ministry is one of the most notable themes of the Gospel narratives. It is a divine reminder that in the Christian life, prayer always precedes activity and that our apostolic endeavours are but the overflow of our interior life. This spiritual edict also stands true for our families, our parishes and our schools. I therefore heartily commend Raymond Friel for authoring the book, *Prayers for Schools*.

As with anybody privileged to proclaim the Gospel, the words and actions of the Catholic teacher have to be consonant with each other. After all, Jesus Christ is not only the Truth, he is also the Way and the Life. Orthodoxy requires orthopraxy and that requires a serious-minded pursuit of holiness, the fullness of Christian life, in the middle of the world. Pope Francis said the following in a memorable audience in November 2014:

It is by living with love and offering Christian witness in our daily tasks that we are called to become saints...Yes, you can! There, where you work you can become a saint. God gives you the grace to become a saint. God communicates with you. Always and everywhere you can become a saint, that is, by being receptive to the grace that is working in us and leads us to holiness.

This, however, can only happen when our interior life is nurtured by private prayer. There is no other starting point, no other route. It is only private prayer that will lead to grounded public prayer that will lead to a Catholic ethos – and a new evangelisation – within our schools.

The result will be Catholic teachers who live servant leadership centred on Jesus Christ. Just as he astonished the crowd by teaching "as one who had authority, and not as their scribes," so too our young people will detect the difference. They too have a nose for the authentic as opposed to the ersatz.

Thus each youthful soul entrusted to our care will also become better equipped to develop a prayer life that will sustain them during their school years and beyond as they continue to draw closer to the loving heart of Our Risen Lord.

+ Leo Cushley
Archbishop of St Andrews & Edinburgh

I

PRAYER:
AN INTRODUCTION
FOR TEACHERS

Lulu's letter

When Lulu was six years old, she
wrote a letter to God. The letter was
short, but asked a very profound
question: "To God, how did you get
invented? From Lulu. x"[1] Lulu asked
her parents to send the letter to God
by setting light to it and putting it up
the chimney, as they did with her
letter to Father Christmas. The dilemma for Lulu's loving parents was that they
did not believe in God, although they indulged their daughter's belief in Father
Christmas. Lulu's father, award-winning journalist Alex Renton, explained that
"I didn't want to tell Lulu there was no God, and I could not tell her there was."[2]

A few months beforehand, not long into the first term at her new school, Lulu's
parents had found their daughter praying at bedtime. They thought this was
rather sweet, to begin with, but then on reflection they decided they were not
entirely happy with this new bedtime routine. They felt that her education had
been taken onto controversial ground without their permission. Lulu didn't need
God to learn to be a good person and she certainly didn't need any threats to
make the right moral choices. With no encouragement from home to think about
God, Renton knew where this interest in the divine was coming from: Lulu's new
school. He admits that he and his wife were ill-informed and had no idea "that a
state primary school affiliated with a church would do quite so much God."[3]

The problem got worse for them when Lulu came home from school and declared
that her grandmother's recently deceased dog was in heaven being looked after
by St Francis of Assisi. Lulu's world view was being shaped in an alarmingly
different way to theirs and they felt they needed to take some action. So when
Lulu wrote her letter to God, they were pleased inasmuch as the question of
God's invention might be the first step to gently disabuse their daughter of her
nascent belief in the supernatural. But rather than sitting her down and
encouraging their daughter back to their own belief, they adopted an impeccably
fair-minded approach. They decided to put Lulu's question to the religious people
who believed in such things, perhaps in the hope that their answers would be
unconvincing. It was their fault, after all, that their daughter had started this
communication with the divine, so let them provide an answer for her.

Alex Renton sent a jpeg of Lulu's letter to all the major Christian denominations in Scotland, where they were based. He got some response, but nothing that really spoke to a six-year-old. For good measure, he had also written to Lambeth Palace, the headquarters of the Church of England. A few weeks later, he got a reply saying that someone special was going to write to Lulu. Eventually an email arrived from "Archbishop Rowan" which contained the following letter:

> Dear Lulu,
>
> Your dad has sent on your letter and asked if I have any answers. It's a difficult one! But I think God might reply a bit like this –
>
> "Dear Lulu – Nobody invented me – but lots of people discovered me and were quite surprised. They discovered me when they looked round at the world and thought it was really beautiful or really mysterious and wondered where it came from. They discovered me when they were very very quiet on their own and felt a sort of peace and love they hadn't expected.
>
> Then they invented ideas about me – some of them sensible and some of them not very sensible. From time to time I sent them some hints – especially in the life of Jesus – to help them get closer to what I'm really like.
>
> But there was nothing and nobody around before me to invent me. Rather like somebody who writes a story in a book, I started making up the story of the world and eventually invented human beings like you who could ask me awkward questions!"
>
> And then he'd send you lots of love and sign off.
>
> I know he doesn't usually write letters, so I have to do the best I can on his behalf. Lots of love from me too.
>
> + Archbishop Rowan[4]

The letter was well received by Alex Renton and Lulu. He explained to her who Rowan Williams was and what he stood for. Lulu was taken by the idea of "God's story". When he reached the end of the letter, her father asked Lulu what she thought. After a while she replied, "Well, I have very different ideas. But he has a good one."[5]

Lessons to be learned

There are several aspects of this delightful story which I think are significant as we look at prayer in school. Firstly, it is remarkable how naturally Lulu began a conversation with God a few weeks after starting at her church school (with the reference to St Francis, I assume it may have been Catholic). Opponents of church schools would say that this is brainwashing. Alex Renton was clearly uncomfortable with what was going on but resisted such easy accusations. The fact is that whatever school a child goes to will have a world view, a set of values and assumptions, based on some foundational belief. There is no such thing as a value-free education. To be educated in a school which clearly has no belief in the divine (an anomaly in historical terms) is to be educated in a value system, to see the world through a particular lens. I have never heard anyone in Catholic or Anglican education saying that such schools should not exist. The argument has always been to let other types of education exist. A liberal democracy should embrace diversity in educational provision, provided there is parental demand and it is within the law.

Secondly, the archbishop illustrates a very important point with his thoughtful and wise letter. In Catholic and Church of England schools, our starting point, our foundational belief, is that God exists, we "do God", as Alex Renton discovered. But how do we talk to today's children (and their parents, who increasingly, like Alex Renton, tick "none" in the Religion box) about God, what kind of language should we use to explain the mystery that is God? Our society is increasingly "tone deaf" to the language and music of the divine. We who work in church schools need to develop an accessible language to engage our young people with the eternal. Rowan Williams points us in the right direction.

Thirdly, the good archbishop exemplifies an important point about leadership: pay attention to the question and take the time to reply. This is challenging but manageable in a school context, but when one is the head of the worldwide Anglican communion, to take the time to reply to a six-year-old is very impressive. I have only met Rowan Williams once, briefly, and was left with the impression of a gentle, holy, scholarly man. It comes as no surprise that he would find the time to reply to Lulu.

The fourth and final lesson to draw from our story is for those engaged in teaching about religion or leading prayer (which in a Catholic or Church of England school will be most teachers) and that is the importance of encouraging questions and dealing sensitively and openly with the answers. In my Catholic upbringing, we were not encouraged to ask questions. There was a body of sacred knowledge, the "deposit of faith", which covered every base and answered every question, so there was no need for questions. In the Catholic Church today, there is much more emphasis on "accompaniment", on journeying with our young people as they engage with questions of belief. In some dioceses 50 per cent and more of the pupils are not Catholic and many of the Catholic children are not practising. In such a context we have to be sensitive to the background of our pupils, many of whom will simply not "get" the language and concepts of religion. This does not mean we compromise on our beliefs and practices, but it does mean that we proceed by "invitation" – offering them this view of the world and witnessing to it – rather than assuming everybody shares our views.

Jesus: the revelation of God

As the letter from Rowan Williams said, the biggest hint about what God is like came in the life, death and resurrection of Jesus. In fact, it was more than a hint. The *Catechism of the Catholic Church* says that in Jesus, the revelation of God is complete: "In him he has said everything; there will be no other word than this one."[6] What we have been doing in the centuries since is trying to grasp the full significance of this remarkable belief, that in Jesus of Nazareth, a first century Jewish preacher and healer, the "inner most being of God"[7] was revealed. It is not that Jesus was an unusually insightful messenger who had special access to the nature of God to pass on. He was God. And man. At the same time. And still is, risen from the dead. This explains the profound and unique relationship between Jesus and his Father: "No-one knows the Son except the Father, just as no-one knows the Father except the Son" (Matthew 11:27).

This also explains why prayer was such a feature of the life of Jesus. As a devout Jew, Jesus would have prayed along with his community in the synagogue and read the scriptures. But in the Gospels we see much more than that. We often see Jesus rising early to go off to a lonely place to pray, or praying all night before a major decision like the choosing of the twelve apostles. In Luke's Gospel it says that Jesus went to pray after the last supper "as usual to the Mount of Olives" (Luke22:39). Also in Luke's Gospel, the transfiguration is presented as a mystical prayer event. Jesus took Peter, James and John up the mountain "to pray" (Luke 9:28). As he prayed, "his face was changed" (9:29) and his clothes became "brilliant as lightning" (9:28). He is transfigured by the love of his Father which is communicated to him in prayer: "This is my Son, the Chosen One" (9:35).

The disciples in the meantime did not always understand what was going on. In the transfiguration scene, Moses and Elijah had also appeared with Jesus and Peter wanted to build a tent for them all, but "he did not know what he was saying" (9:33). The disciples' experience of prayer as Jews was clearly different to what they witnessed in Jesus. He prayed differently, intensely, in a way which was everything to do with his relationship to his Father. In another scene in Luke's Gospel, it says that when Jesus had finished praying (clearly they weren't praying with him), one of the disciples said to him, "Lord, teach us to pray, just as John taught his disciples" (Luke 11:1). I don't know if there was a little barb in there: John taught his disciples to pray, but you don't seem to have got round to that part of our induction programme yet.

Our Father

In response to this request, barbed or not, Jesus teaches his disciples the most famous of all Christian prayers, the Our Father. Luke's version is shorter than Matthew's, it's more direct and more likely to be very close to the words used by Jesus, preserved in memory and committed to writing by the evangelist Luke around fifty years after the death of Jesus:

> Father, may your name be held holy,
> Your kingdom come;
> Give us each day our daily bread
> And forgive us our sins,
> For we ourselves forgive each one who is in debt to us.
> And do not put us to the test.
>
> (Luke 11:2-4)

Jesus goes on to give them further advice about persisting in prayer, like a man whose friend turns up in the night and he has to wake a neighbour to get some food. He tells his disciples to "ask, and it will be given to you; search and you will find" (Luke 11:9). He uses the very down to earth and touching image of a son asking his father for bread and "what father among you would hand his son a stone when he asked for bread" (Luke 11:11). We should be careful not to interpret this as Jesus saying whatever you ask for in prayer will be granted. This could lead to a greedy approach, with people assailing heaven for new iPhones and top grades in exams. That's not what Jesus is saying here. If you read on, the point is that God will respond to prayer with what you need, with what is good for you, which is the Holy Spirit.

The Our Father has had a very special place in the Christian tradition from the earliest days of the Church. *The Didache*, which is a kind of early Church manual, written around the beginning of the second century, includes Matthew's longer version of the Our Father, with the instruction to "say this prayer three times a day."[8] It is also interesting to note as an aside that Wednesday and Friday are identified as fast days. We've largely lost the habit of fasting since then. However, if in your school you are praying three times a day (morning prayer, at midday, and at the end of the day) then you are part of a very long tradition. It is worth paying some attention to the Our Father and examining what it tells us about prayer and Jesus' understanding of his Father in heaven.

Friends of God

Rowan Williams writes that because of Jesus Christ "we could talk to God in a different way."[9] In the Old Testament God was not entirely a figure of wrath and thunder, but he was seen as radically "other" and remote. The Jewish people had a great regard for the name of God given to Moses, *YHWH*. They would not even pronounce this out loud, such was their reverence. They used circumlocutions like *Adonai*. The name YHWH was uttered once a year by the high priest in the holy of holies in the temple, but the choir soared to drown him out. For Jesus to start his prayer with the familiar "Father", one who is in intimate relationship with us, was a remarkable departure from the religious culture of his time. Williams goes on to say that, "Very near to the heart of Christian prayer is getting over the idea that God is somewhere a very, very long way off, so that we have to shout loudly to be heard. On the contrary: God has decided to be an intimate friend and he has decided to make us part of the family, and we always pray on that basis."[10] This is such an important point to stress when we are praying with pupils. God is very close to us.

In fact, in the earliest writing following the death of Jesus, which was not the Gospels, but the letters of St Paul, the thought is developed that God is present *in us*, in the form of his Spirit. In his letter to the young church in Galatia, written perhaps only twenty years after the death of Jesus, St Paul tells them that "God has sent the Spirit of his Son into our hearts, crying, 'Abba, Father' so you are no longer a slave but a child, and if a child then also an heir, through God" (Galatians 4:6). This remarkable insight is crucial when we are talking about prayer. It is important that in some way we share this with our pupils. The point is that it is not really us who are doing the praying. It's not in fact something that requires our skill, like playing football or netball. In a strange way, this takes the pressure off. The Spirit of God will do all the work, all we have to do is get out of the way. YOUCAT, the *Youth Catechism of the Catholic Church*, expresses it in this way, "This Holy Spirit of Jesus is in us, and he is speaking through us when we pray. Basically prayer means that from the depth of my heart, God speaks to God."[11]

So where does this leave those who pray? Are we simply some kind of ventriloquist's dummy made to speak in the voice of God? Well, not quite. We have the freedom to be open or not to this Spirit of Jesus in us. We have to allow the Spirit in us to communicate with God. We can block that, with care and anxiety, or indifference. We can allow it to happen by being open and prayerful. Jesus teaches us that using honest and heartfelt words is a very important part of prayer, like a simple "Father!" After the very familiar opening to the Our Father in Luke's Gospel, Jesus says, "your kingdom come" (Luke 11:2). We are asking for the world to be transformed: may what God wants shine through in the world, may the way God sees things be the way we see things. We then ask for daily bread, but we are not just talking about ourselves, the prayer says give "us" our daily bread. YOUCAT says that "no Christian can pronounce this petition without thinking about his real responsibility for those in the world who lack the basic necessities of life."[12] So right from the beginning of the Christian prayer tradition we are praying for other people and a just arrangement of the goods of the earth.

We are also praying for forgiveness, another core Christian theme. The way it is expressed in the Our Father has sounded to some people like a harsh deal. God will not forgive us unless we forgive other people. That does seem very demanding, since we probably all have somebody in our life that we will struggle to forgive. So what is the point of this part of the prayer? YOUCAT says that, "If we ourselves are not merciful and do not forgive one another, God's mercy will not reach our hearts."[13] That to me is a much more helpful and psychologically convincing formula. If we are locked into a state of un-forgiveness (like the elder son at the end of the story of the prodigal son, Luke 15:25-32) then we will not be able to *receive* the forgiveness of God which is readily available. If we are in a "deep blockade of being unreconciled"[14] to our neighbour then we prevent the forgiveness of God from getting through. Forgiving someone is like opening a channel, or to use another image from the Gospels, "loosing" us from a burden. Mercy can then flow in both directions.

Characteristics of prayer

In our prayers in schools, these are some of our foundational principles, given to us directly by Jesus in the prayer he taught us. God is a father who is very close to us and only wants what is good for us. What is good for us is the Spirit of Jesus living in us and guiding us towards the love of the Father. The "kingdom" which began with the life of Jesus and which is still unfolding, slowly but surely, is a vision of life in which the gentle ways of God are the norm, not the competitive ways of human beings. Relationships in this kingdom are understood in a different way. We are invited to be reconciled to each other, to ensure that no-one is a victim or in a state of want, either physically, emotionally or spiritually. In fact, relationships are so central to our relationships with God that in Matthew's Gospel Jesus tells us that if we are not at peace with our neighbour, then go and sort it out before we start to pray: "if you are bringing your offering to the altar and there remember that your brother has something against you, leave your offering there before the altar, go and be reconciled with your brother first, and then come back and present your offering" (Matthew 5:23-25).

From this we can see that prayer is not just about us and it's not about a performance to impress a divine examiner. God knows us and doesn't ask for much from us. He just wants us to come to him in prayer. In Luke's Gospel Jesus tells a wonderful story to some people "who trusted in themselves that they were righteous and regarded others with contempt" (Luke 18:9). When Jesus wanted to make a point about behaviour which was not acceptable in the eyes of God, he often told a story. I would love to have been there sometimes when the penny dropped. A Pharisee (a kind of professional religious lay person) and a tax collector, who was regarded as a sinner and despised by the community, both went to the temple to pray. The Pharisee was full of pride for his religious accomplishments in fasting and prayer. He compared himself most favourably to the tax collector, who in the meantime only had this to say: "God, be merciful to me a sinner" (Luke 18:14). All he brought to his prayers was humility, a sense of his own unworthiness before God. And which of the two, according to Jesus, was "justified" (18:14)? The tax collector.

So when we come to pray, we shouldn't feel any pressure to feel "holy" or boast about our virtues or great acts of religion. We've already heard that one of the first great insights of the Christian tradition is that God's spirit is within us, praying for us. What we have to do is to get our ego, our selfishness and self-obsession, out of the way. Jesus does give some further advice in Matthew's Gospel about where and how to pray. He makes it clear that praying to show off in front of others is not the point. He recommends that we go to a private place and "do not heap up empty phrases as the Gentiles do" (6:7). Jesus is not against public prayers, but is against trying to manipulate God and make him like us with long impressive ritualistic prayers. It seems to be much simpler than that. It's about responding to God's invitation to get to know him, to be a friend, to let his Spirit grow in us.

Over the years, we have thought a great deal about God and prayer. Our most brilliant theologians have come up with sophisticated proofs of God's existence and written very long books about prayer, grace, salvation, redemption. And that work is important. We need to use our human faculties to try and understand the mystery of God's revelation, but we must never lose sight of the fact that at the very heart of divine revelation is a remarkably simple insight: God loves you and wants you to love him. God is not some stern figure who is waiting to be impressed by your virtue and prayers. In the Catechism of the Catholic Church it says that it is God "who first seeks us."[15] Referring to the story in John's Gospel when Jesus meets the woman at the well and asks her for a drink (see: Lent prayer), it says that, "Jesus thirsts; his asking arises from the depths of God's desire for us."[16] This is good news. This is a message that children are perhaps more receptive to than adults. We are invited to be child-like in the face of this great invitation from God.

We pray because God, the creator of life, wants us to get to know him in the depths of our hearts. We pray because it's natural. We have deep within us a sense of the presence of God and we will not be entirely happy until we are at one with that presence. For many people this is experienced as "something missing" in life, a vacuum, a gap. We pray because we can't rely on ourselves. Prayer is being present to this loving divine reality, recognising our profound need; in the words of the Catechism, "the raising of one's mind and heart to God."[17] And how do we pray? Well, we can use words, directed to our Father. Not too many words and not words for the sake of it, but honest words, asking for what we need. Our prayers are always directed *to* the Father, *through* Jesus Christ, *in* the Holy Spirit.

Prayer can also be silence and many believe that this is the best way to pray, just being silent in the presence of God. This is not always easy and sometimes we need our words and imagination to help us understand what is going on in our world. But those I have spoken to in schools tell me that children and young people take to silent prayer remarkably quickly (see: Part III). And how often do we pray? As we've noticed already, the earliest advice was to pray three times a day. The first monks in the Egyptian desert took St Paul's advice to "pray constantly" (1 Thessalonians 5:18) quite literally and prayed a lot. But the basic advice about prayer throughout the Christian tradition is that it is "daily bread" and it should be a daily habit. If you have a true friend, you wouldn't just turn to them when you were in trouble. Friendship develops by spending time with each other, through good days and bad, in other words by being faithful.

Five types of prayer

Over the years, Christians have developed many different prayers and ways of praying because it can take us a while to trust silence, and people at different times and in different cultures have a variety of needs and priorities. We've also come to learn that at times in our life, in different seasons and moods, our prayers can take on a certain character. Sometimes we're angry with God and just need to get it out, sometimes we're really worried about someone else and we naturally turn to God for help. Sometimes we feel the need for blessing, to know we are loved. Sometimes we are lost in the wonder and beauty of life and just want to praise God, or else we're overcome with gratitude for what we've got and just want to say thank you. In the Catholic tradition, there are five main types of prayer. It's good for pupils to know what they are so they can understand the different ways in which they can pray, although as we'll see later, they are often there ahead of us.

Blessing and adoration

A blessing is something good that comes from God. YOUCAT describes blessing as a message from God as follows: "God the Father and Creator of all being says: It is good that you exist. The fact that you are is something beautiful."[18] All of our pupils, indeed all of our staff, need to hear that message: *it is good that you exist.* So many of our young people are struggling with low self-esteem and image problems. They don't always hear that message even from their own parents, who have the same issues, or who don't have the time or emotional capacity to tell their children that it is good that they are on this earth, that they are beautiful. A prayer of blessing is a prayer that calls down God's blessing upon us. "From God alone all blessings flow. His goodness, his closeness, his mercy – that is blessing,"[19] says YOUCAT. Every Christian is invited to call down God's blessing on themselves and other people. Those who love each other can bless each other.

In the Catholic tradition, the priest blesses explicitly in the name of Jesus and on behalf of the Church. His request for blessings comes with the prayer power of the whole Church. I have experienced that on a number of special occasions, either at Mass, or in confession – *being placed under the blessing of the Church*. It is a powerful reminder and recognition of the beauty of our existence and the fact that we are loved by our creator. In my upbringing, the blessing of objects was common. Houses were blessed, new cars, rosaries, Bibles. It can become ritualistic and superstitious if you end up thinking that harm will come to this house until it is blessed, but the basic instinct is theologically sound: ask for God's blessing to make a good home, to travel safely, to pray well.

Adoration of God is a natural consequence of understanding that we are God's creation, his creatures, and we owe our very existence to him. Christian adoration recognises the holiness and mystery of God and kneels before the divine love that became human in Jesus Christ. Christians have always shown their reverence for God by kneeling in prayer, or prostrating themselves on the ground. This expresses our relationship to the divine mystery. We are so fragile and needy before God and yet we have this remarkable revelation in the Gospels that we are friends of God. Despite our smallness, we are loved and cherished by God. This sense of the sacred is something which our society has all but lost. In a world in which self-reliance is constantly promoted, the postures and gestures of adoration are seen as strange and subservient. In the Catholic Church, we are beginning to see a return to this sense of reverence, with people genuflecting before they receive communion and a revived devotion to the Blessed Sacrament (see Part III).

Petition

The prayer of petition is when we turn to God in our need. The traditional posture for prayers of petition is hands joined, or folded. God already knows what we need but nevertheless, says YOUCAT, "God wants us to ask, to turn to him in times of need, to cry out, implore, lament, call upon him, indeed even struggle with him in prayer."[20] God does not need our petitions to know what we need. YOUCAT offers the insight that, "someone who does not ask and does not want to ask shuts himself up in himself."[21] We become our own horizon if we're not in communication with the divine. As Lulu discovered, it is very natural to talk to God. It is also reassuring to hear that when we talk to God we do not have to be on our best behaviour. We don't need to sound pious or tell God what we think he wants to hear, as if we're talking to an Ofsted inspector. We're invited to talk to God openly and honestly, no matter what mood we're in or how good or bad we feel. This is important to remember when the pupils are writing their own prayers, or praying spontaneously: they should be themselves and be allowed to express the full range of emotions and frustrations.

Indeed, that's exactly what we find in the Bible. Denis McBride, a Redemptorist priest and scripture scholar, notes that "prayers of lamentation form the largest category of the psalms. They are cries from the heart, shouts of suffering, groans of anguish, screams for help, protests against what is happening. They are written on a bed of pain in the hope that God or someone will listen and intervene."[22] This outpouring of petition has a psychological and sociological dimension as well. Through articulation of suffering, people can come to an awareness of the suffering that can be changed and the suffering that has to be accepted. McBride notes that "there is much avoidable suffering that is permitted to thrive through apathy."[23] There is also suffering which cannot be avoided and this is what often produces the most heart-breaking petition. In the suffering of Jesus, we see one of the most poignant examples of this. In his darkest hour, abandoned to pain and public ridicule on the cross, Jesus prayed the words of Psalm 22, "My God, my God, why have you deserted me?" (Mark 15:34). At this moment, we see Jesus in the very depth of the human condition. He did not just experience the best bits of being human. "All the despair, all the laments, all the cries of mankind in all times, and yearning for God's helping hand are contained in this word of the Crucified."[24] Sometimes, it's only on the morning of resurrection that our prayers are answered.

Intercession

People have a deep instinct to pray for other people, especially in a time of need. This is the prayer of intercession. Even in our society, as secular as it is, we often hear public figures saying "my thoughts and prayers are with you at this time." This has drawn criticism from the atheist lobby who then ask, "what does that mean?" and regard the sentiment almost as an insult. But there is a very long biblical tradition of prayers of intercession, going back to Abraham who bargained with God to save the just men of Sodom, and God agreed (Genesis 18:16-33). This brings us back to the question we considered regarding petitions: does God answer our prayers for others? When Jesus comes back down the mountain after the transfiguration scene in Luke's Gospel, he is met by a man who pleads for his only son who is possessed by a spirit who sends the boy into convulsions (in all probability the boy was epileptic). The boy is "disfigured" by this possession, brought upon him by the sins of his ancestors, as was the belief. Jesus, the "transfigured" son, heals the boy and gives him back to his father.

There are many other examples of Jesus answering petitions for sick relatives in the Gospels, so why is every prayer for healing not answered? We also have a long tradition in the Catholic Church of asking Mary, the Mother of God, and the saints, to pray for us. We do not pray to them: that would be idolatry. We ask them to pray on our behalf, since they are close to God. Again, some prayers appear to be answered, some not. Well, God is not an ATM: we put the prayer card in, we get the answer we want out. YOUCAT says that "we must leave it up to him how he will answer our petitions."[25] Why do some of the prayers of good people seem to go unheeded? Why do some of the prayers of the desperate seem to fall on deaf ears? Why do some bad people seem to prosper? The truth is we do not fully know the mind of God. It takes us back to the point we made earlier that to pray for a certain outcome, or to pray that history is bent to our will, is perhaps not what we should be praying for, rather we should be praying to be "possessed" more and more by God's transforming Holy Spirit.

We pray for others, as we should, but not as a kind of spiritual lottery, hoping that soon it will be our turn to hit the jackpot and get exactly what we've prayed for. Praying for the needs of others reminds me that I am part of a spiritual family which is more than just my nearest and dearest. Jesus made the old law of love of God and neighbour more radical by insisting that we should love our enemies. If we love our enemies, then we should pray for them too. Pope Francis, in his apostolic exhortation, *The Joy of the Gospel*, reminded us that "contemplation always has a place for others."[26] The letters of St Paul are full of prayers for others, by name. This attitude to prayer reminds us that we are not on a private escalator to heaven, it's not just about saving our soul, it's about God and neighbour. Prayers of intercession help us to be grateful for others, to be attentive to them and to see how God is working in their lives. It also frees us from selfishness. Pope Francis says that when Christians rise from prayers of intercession "their hearts are more open; freed of self-absorption… desirous of doing good and sharing their lives with others."[27]

Thanksgiving

The fourth main type of prayer recognised in the Catechism is prayer of thanksgiving. This prayer seems straightforward in the sense that we all have an intuition that there is a need to say "thank you" when we receive something good, especially if the giving is gratuitous, nothing is expected in return, no strings attached, no return invite required. As parents, we often used the phrase, "now what do you say?" when our children received something from grannie and forgot to say thank you.

In Luke's Gospel, when Jesus heals ten lepers, he makes the point that only one comes back to say thank you. Prayers of thanksgiving are a recognition that "everything that we are and have comes from God."[28] Our life comes from God and our redemption comes from God, in Jesus. Before he became a human being, we had an incomplete understanding of the way to the Father. We did not know that this God of the universe was simply love and was going to be revealed, not as a political liberator, but as a forgiving victim. The way to the Father is through faith – humble, open, trusting, transforming faith – and reaching out to the victims of the world.

Praise

This is why the fifth type of prayer is the prayer of praise. We need to express spontaneously and in liturgy our delight that God *is* and that we have the opportunity to enter into a relationship of intimacy with him. Praise is perhaps the "purest" form of prayer, the most disinterested. Our prayers are often mixed with self-interest, perhaps in ways that we are not even aware of, but praise to God is offered with no expectation of anything in return. For that reason, it is perhaps the type of prayer that offers the least room for creativity. We can think of endless blessings, petitions, intercessions and reasons to be grateful, but praise is praise, pure and simple. We join with the angels and saints in heaven in their eternal praise. The posture most associated with praise is hands and arms outstretched (the Orans or Orante posture). In the Catholic tradition, at least in Britain, our arms don't leave our sides very often when we pray, perhaps just for the sign of the cross, or sign of peace. Culturally, we are quite reserved, although that is changing. In other cultures and in other places in the Church, such as the Charismatic movement, we see much greater freedom to praise God by holding up our arms.

I remember going to the Flame conference in London with our pupils a few years ago. Flame is perhaps the biggest gathering of young Catholics in Britain. They come together to pray, sing and praise. When Matt Redman opened the conference with "Bless my Soul" everybody was on their feet with arms aloft. As one of the small cohort of the middle-aged at this gathering I managed to get to my feet but struggled to move my arms away from my sides. After a few songs, however, and realising that nobody cared less, I found the freedom to praise God in song and gesture, getting my arms up in the air. It was immensely enjoyable and liberating. We do need to pray with our bodies. This is much more difficult in school and it depends on the school's culture, but it's worth remembering that praise of our God is not something that can be muttered into a desk, it is the work of body and soul.

What's the point of prayer?

We've heard that prayer is a turning of our attention to God, which is natural for human beings who have a God-shaped hole in their soul, a piece missing from the programme. Our hearts are restless until they rest in God. We've looked at the different types of prayer in the Christian tradition and how they reflect the variety of human experience and the nature of our relationship with God. So if a pupil asks, "after all this praying, miss, what's supposed to be happening?" what do we tell them? It's a fair question and the answer could be something along the lines that we pray so that we can become closer to God, more like God. We pray in other words so that we will be *transformed*, from selfish into selfless people, from cold into compassionate people, from small souls into big souls, literally *magnanimous* human beings. And it is not a private project. We are members of the greater family of the body of Christ and if we are on a journey to holiness, that inevitably means that we are more attentive to our neighbour and our environment, more caring, more determined to seek justice for the oppressed and more inclined to forgive than to hang on to our grievances.

Rowan Williams says that "prayer is about reconciliation, justice, and how it changes your attitude to other people and the world. Prayer is not a narrowly private activity; it is about belonging in the body of Christ and in the family of humanity."[29] So it's about us being transformed and in turn seeking to transform the world for the better. This is the building up of the kingdom, the task which Jesus entrusted to his disciples. At Pentecost, he sent them his Holy Spirit to inspire this apostolic, missionary effort. Prayer of course is not the only means by which we can grow in grace, or holiness. The Catholic Church is very clear that the sacraments, especially the Eucharist, and the word of God are two principal means by which the faithful encounter the grace of God, but that would be another book.

The youth of today

Having said all that, are today's young people at all interested in any of this? A few points to consider. In a Catholic or Church of England school, we do not say prayers because the pupils want to, we say them because our schools are Christian communities and praying is one of the defining characteristics of a Christian community. In the Acts of the Apostles, Luke describes the features of the earliest Christian community as follows: "They remained faithful to the teaching of the apostles, to the brotherhood, to the breaking of bread and to the prayers" (Acts 2:42). There is also the small matter of the law. The far-sighted 1944 Education Act introduced the requirement for schools in England and Wales to hold a daily act of collective worship, broadly Christian in character. In Scotland and Northern Ireland the law requires a daily act of religious observance. Subsequent education acts in England have modified the requirement but it has never been repealed. Ofsted used to report on compliance with this requirement but in the face of widespread breaches, the monitoring was quietly dropped. The fact that most schools without a religious character ignore the requirement does not change the fact that the law remains.

In England and Wales, parents have the right to withdraw their children from the collective worship and if they are over sixteen pupils can withdraw themselves. In my experience, in both Catholic and Church of England schools, this rarely happened. As I noted already, not all pupils in Catholic or Church of England schools are Catholic or Anglican, but they are in school communities where an essential part of the life of the community is the saying of prayers. There are a growing number of Muslim children in Catholic schools, some 20,000 at the last census, because they value a school environment where religion, the ways of God and prayer, are taken seriously. These children take part in the prayers of the Christian community. One of the more notable features of our schools is that every day hundreds of thousands of young people (in Catholic schools over 800,000) *pray*. It is a striking counter-cultural witness in this so-called secular society.

In a school culture where praying is the norm, it has always struck me how easily young people take to it. I have seen classrooms of sixteen-year-olds engaged in writing prayers for Lent and happy to read them out at Mass and in assembly. Because of the culture they were in they had "permission" to pray and to write prayers. Nobody thought they were weird, there was no peer pressure, it was the norm. The pupils, Catholic or Christian or not, enjoyed the opportunity to communicate with the divine, as Lulu did at the beginning of her education. The humanist lobby consider this to be unacceptable brainwashing. The more extreme voices in the humanist lobby would even call it child abuse. I would counter that by saying that to deny a child the opportunity to communicate with God is a privation, a diminishment of their humanity.

Today's young people are sometimes accused by their elders of being the most spoiled generation in history: materialistic, shallow and selfish, with no respect for manners or tradition. There is some compelling evidence to the contrary. In a recent Youth for Christ survey of 1,001 11-18-year-olds,[30] 82 per cent said that their most important priority was "Making my Family Proud of Me". The next two were "Feeling That I Have Achieved Something That Matters" and "Becoming a Better Person". Only then came "Becoming Successful" (64 per cent) and "Money" (62 per cent). The survey confirms what many of our teachers know already, that while our young people are in and of the culture and share many of its aspirations for material success, there is a strong moral dimension to their outlook and a desire to do something worthwhile with their lives.

What the 11-18 age group were most anxious about would come as little surprise to those who work in schools. The biggest concern (54 per cent) was "Schools and Exams", followed by "Appearance" (30 per cent) and "What People Think of Me" (30 per cent). Some of the prayers in this book are written with those concerns in mind (see: "On a mufti day – how do I look?"). Time spent online is now habitual: 72 per cent of young people go on the internet daily, with 94 per cent at least once a week. When you consider that in the light of their concerns, you can see how social media is one of the greatest sources of anxiety, with relentless messages about body shape and size, "body shaming", and a new culture of unrestricted, often abusive, expression (see: "Safer internet day"). When it comes to Religion and Faith, 47 per cent said they don't believe in God, which almost matches the current figures of "no religion" in the wider society; 32 per cent said they did believe in God (21 per cent don't know) and of that group, 41 per cent said they prayed. Over half of young people who said they believed in God did not develop that relationship through prayer, whereas 47 per cent of those who said they did pray, prayed once a day.

In the course of preparing this book, I had the privilege of interviewing groups of pupils at Abbey Catholic Primary School in Birmingham and St Thomas More Catholic High School in Crewe. The pupils were a genuine reflection of their school communities and not just the ones who would tell the nice visitor what he wanted to hear about prayers in school. In my years of headship, I always enjoyed talking to pupils, listening to their stories. They have a depth of spirituality which we can so easily overlook. It is no accident that Jesus in the Gospels often presents children as exemplars of proximity to God: they are more open and trusting, not yet completely saddened and hardened by the world. In the Abbey School, one pupil said that prayer was when they "calmed down to think about God and what we've been given." Prayer was about thanking God and asking for his forgiveness. Prayer should be peaceful, they said, like when we know we're forgiven. I asked the pupils if we should always get what we ask for in prayer. One of the pupils, aged ten, said, "It depends if it's something you want, or something you need, is it very necessary." I don't know if the pupils had been briefed on the five types of prayer, but they had an unerring instinct about what they were and a deep appreciation of prayer.

In St Thomas More, with a group of 11-15-year-olds, I found a similar level of spiritual engagement. There were some interesting comments that formal prayers were not helpful, that prayers should be personal, concerned with what the pupils wanted to say. This was countered with some very insightful comments about crisis moments in life, like bereavement, when we need to have prayers we can say, familiar prayers of the Church which bring comfort. The pupils felt that prayer was about connecting with God and being thankful. One pupil called prayer like being in a conversation with God throughout the day. He's always there, next to you, he's not hiding. One pupil said that God talks back to you without talking, by spiritually offering comfort. Another pupil developed the point and said God talks to you though your conscience, in how you feel about things. They all felt that in their school belief was not forced on them. They talked about the peer pressure they felt from friends outside of school, and of how being in their school gave them the strength to stand up for what they believed in. One girl spoke movingly about the sense of wonder she felt just looking up at the stars. "We've been given that," she said. Adults are there to teach and guide children, but we must never assume that we have nothing to learn from them.

Prayers for schools

Our young people, despite the enormous pressure from a secular society, have not turned their back on God completely and have not turned their back on living an altruistic life. Our "faith" schools, as they are called, are not scattering seed on thin soil, as some people today believe. Within the Catholic Church there are some who say that Catholic schools have diluted their ethos over the years in order to accommodate secular expectations. This is certainly not my experience. When I attended a Catholic primary school in Scotland in the late 1960s/early 1970s, much was taken for granted about the Catholic life of the pupils. We lived in a Catholic culture, in which priest-filled parishes and Catholic families were part of a trinity of Catholic life, along with the schools. We prayed in the Catholic tradition, were prepared for the sacraments and gave money to charity, although the "missions" were presented in a very patronising way. Much was taken for granted in this Catholic culture. It was the air we breathed.

However, there was no real imaginative engagement with the lives and experiences of the pupils and how prayer life might be adapted to speak to them in a language they understood. When I visit schools today I am always struck by the imaginative depth of the prayer and liturgical life of the schools. Yes, we have a wealth of resources in the Christian tradition, but much of it is simply not accessible to young people (or, increasingly, their parents). Much of the language does not make sense to them. We need to find new and imaginative ways to introduce our young people to the great news of salvation, as Rowan Williams tried to do for Lulu. This book is an attempt to contribute to those resources: to try and help our teachers to understand what prayer is, to present some original prayers which hopefully will introduce our young people to key moments in the great story of the Good News while also addressing some of their concerns, and provide schools with some helpful case studies from other schools and some tips about being creative in prayer.

The prayers in this book can be used by teachers to support their daily act of collective worship. Practice and policy will vary from school to school but I know all too well that in the hectic life of a school, with more pressure to increase time for the "core" curriculum (i.e. whatever is examined and counts in league tables) the temptation is to reduce time for prayer. We have developed our prayer and liturgical life so much in recent years and we must not let external pressures erode what is at the heart of our schools. My invitation to all our teachers and senior staff is to make sure that we take time for prayer, take time for silence, take God's time. I also hope that these prayers and reflections will inspire pupils and staff to write their own prayers for use in school and indeed at home.

Some of the prayers in this book are long, deliberately so, to encourage reflection and engagement. The prayers can act as a kind of instruction (or induction), supporting the work of Religious Education in outlining some of the main events and ideas in the life of Jesus and the Church. In Part II, I have followed the structure of the school and liturgical year. In the Church's year, the whole plan of salvation is presented, from the early weeks of Advent, through the Nativity, to Lent, the Sacred Triduum and then Ascension and Pentecost. I have also included some prayers for key moments and themes which I know from my experience in schools are of such importance, like the beginning and end of term, beginning and end of the week, plus some key moments from the wider calendar which are important to attend to, such as Holocaust Memorial Day and Martin Luther King Day.

You may wish to stay with one prayer for a week and come back to it for reflection and discussion. Teachers could have a phrase from one of the prayers up on the whiteboard to prompt discussion, such as, "Help us to understand *gift* in a different way, in a different currency, like time, or presence, or prayer" (from "Advent: first week") as the pupils begin to reflect on Advent in the midst of a materialistic culture. You may also like to consider some of the creative ideas for prayer in Part III which I have gleaned from many other schools, with particular thanks to my friend and inspiration Sr Judith Russi for a wealth of ideas. These ways to pray could be used in conjunction with the prayers in Part II, or instead of them. Nor am I suggesting for a moment that we abandon the traditional prayers of the Church. I have referenced some of the main traditional practices in Part III and an excellent compendium of traditional prayers can be found on the website of the Liturgy Office of the Catholic Church in England and Wales: http://www.liturgyoffice.org.uk/ Prayer/Traditional/index.shtml. Teachers are the best judge of which prayers their pupils will be able to access, and as we've heard, the pupils themselves have a sound instinct for when different types of prayer are needed.

It is of course important to follow whatever your school or diocese sets out in its collective worship policy. In my experience, however, there are very few schools or dioceses which dictate which prayers should be said on which days through the year, hence the perennial search for prayers and resources. What may be set out in a policy is a prescribed format, or minimum expectation of content. Many of the prayers in this book are also suitable for use in staff meetings and briefings as well as assemblies. Whatever your practice, I hope that these prayers and ideas can contribute to the prayer life of your schools and help your pupils and staff to grow in the love and friendship of God.

[1] http://rowanwilliams.archbishopofcanterbury.org/articles.php/2389/the-archbishop-writes-to-lulu-aged-6-about-god, accessed 11 July 2017.

[2] Ibid.

[3] Ibid.

[4] Ibid.

[5] Ibid.

[6] *Catechism of the Catholic Church*, 65, http://www.vatican.va/archive/ccc_css/archive/catechism/p1s1c2a1.htm, accessed 13 July 2017.

[7] *Dei Verbum*, Second Vatican Council, 4.

[8] *Early Christian Writings* (London: Penguin Classics, 1987), 194.

[9] Rowan Williams, *Being Christian* (London: SPCK, 2014), 62.

[10] Ibid., 66.

[11] *YOUCAT: Youth Catechism of the Catholic Church* (San Francisco: Ignatius Press, 2011), 272.

[12] Ibid., 284.

[13] Ibid., 286.

[14] Ibid.

[15] CCC, 2560.

[16] Ibid.

[17] Ibid., 2559.

[18] YOUCAT, 104.

[19] Ibid., 266.

[20] Ibid.

[21] Ibid.

[22] Denis McBride, C. Ss. R., *Jesus and the Gospels* (Chawton: Redemptorist Publications, 2006), 138.

[23] Ibid., 139.

[24] YOUCAT, 262.

[25] Ibid.

[26] Pope Francis, *The Joy of the Gospel* (London: Catholic Truth Society, 2013), 281.

[27] Ibid., 282.

[28] YOUCAT, 269.

[29] *Being Christian*, 73.

[30] Youth for Christ, *Gen Z: Rethinking our Culture* (Halesowen: Youth for Christ, 2017).

II

PRAYERS THROUGHOUT THE SCHOOL AND LITURGICAL YEAR

In the name of the Father

And of the Son

And of the

Holy Spirit

Sign of the Cross

In the name of the Father

Who made me

Who made all things wonderfully well

Who is love

And of the Son

Who saves me

Who saves us all from darkness

Who is our teacher

And of the Holy Spirit

Who inspires me

Who inspires us all to live well

Who is our guide

Amen

Amen

Tips for teachers

With new intakes of pupils, more and more will have no grounding in the Catholic Christian faith. When I was a headteacher, the first thing I had to do with the new Year 7 intake was teach them the sign of the cross. Many had never made this gesture in their lives. This prayer may help to unpack a little what we're saying when we address the Trinity. The prayer could be said with one "lead" voice and the part in italics by the rest of the group.

Our Father

Our Father
> *Not a frightening God*
> *But the loving Father of all humanity*

Who art in heaven
> *Not far away but very close*
> *Heaven is where we find the presence of God*

Hallowed be thy name
> *We place your name above all other names*
> *We praise you, we honour you, we thank you*

Thy kingdom come
> *May the world look like the kind of place*
> *God wants it to be, just and compassionate*

Thy will be done on earth as it is in heaven
> *We all want different things*
> *But it's what you want for us and the world that matters*

Give us this day our daily bread
> *Give everybody what they need to live, physically and spiritually,*
> *Give us the grace to help them*

And forgive us our trespasses as we forgive those who trespass against us
> *If we don't forgive other people*
> *We won't be able to feel forgiven*

And lead us not into temptation
> *Protect us from the glamorous path*
> *The world sets before us*

But deliver us from evil
> *Spare us from the terrible things human beings are capable of*
> *and help us to stand against evil in our world when we can*

For thine is the kingdom and the power and the glory, for ever and ever*
> *And your kingdom is loving, your power is gentle and your glory*
> *is humble.*

Amen.
> *Let all this be so.*

*This is usually not said in Catholic communities
but is said in Church of England communities.

At the beginning of term

Loving God,
Another term begins and we come back to school
Refreshed and restored by the break,
Grateful for those we share our lives with,
For the memories of the past few weeks,
For the opportunities we have, which are denied
To so many in our world today.

We come back to school pleased to see our friends,
Determined to make the most of our talents,
To grow in understanding of the kind of person we are called to be,
To turn over a new leaf, perhaps,
To make up for the times we were less than our best self.
We come back to school and are grateful
For the energy and enthusiasm a new term brings,
For the optimism and good humour in the air.

Bless our school, keep us safe and well,
Keep us on the right path.
Bless our teachers and support staff
Who look after us and help us to grow in knowledge and skills.
Bless the new pupils and staff
As they begin their journey with us,
May they very quickly feel at home.
Bless all our efforts to build up the kingdom of God,
To make the world more just and compassionate
Beginning here, in this school of ours,
Our home from home.

Monday morning Examen*

Loving Father,
As we gather together at the beginning
Of another week in school,
We ask for stillness and peace of mind.
We become aware of our breathing,
The breath of life in us, our heartbeat.
We become aware of this precious moment.
There is no other moment more perfect than this one.
Help us to be aware of your loving presence
In our hearts, in our school, in our world.

We look back over our weekend with thanks –
For the family and friends we spent time with,
For what we received from them, for what we gave them,
For the work we did, the rest we enjoyed, the fun we had.
Help us to consider honestly the emotions we felt in the last few days.
What is God trying to tell us in these feelings?
Am I concerned about a friend, a parent, my work in school?
About the things I have and don't have?
Should I be doing something differently because of these feelings?

Let us ask God's Holy Spirit to guide us
And concentrate now on one moment, one encounter
Over the weekend. Let us pray about that moment –
It could be a prayer of blessing, petition,
Intercession for somebody else, thanksgiving, praise.
It could be something we have to say sorry for, to learn from,
To let go of and move on.

Let us now look forward to the day and week ahead.
Help us, loving Father, to keep trying to be better people,
To be positive in our lessons, helpful around school
And kind to everybody we meet.
Help us not to become too anxious about anything
But to trust in you in all things.

We make this our prayer through Christ our Lord.
Amen.

*See: Part III for
more information
on the Examen.

Silence

An introduction to Centering Prayer*

Our world is full of continual distraction -
Our attention is demanded by a thousand pop-ups,
Messages, photos, videos, alerts;
We no longer hear the sound of silence,
Where God can be found.
Let us enter into silence today,
Set aside our anxieties, the to do list,
The conversations that run in our head,
Set aside our ego and its concerns
About what to say, how we have to look,
Who has offended us, who likes us,
Let go of all that and just sit in silence
With the loving presence of the Holy Spirit
Who dwells in us, if we could but listen
And be attentive to his presence.

Loving God, help us to set aside, for a few moments,
The targets, the action plans, the even better ifs,
And just be ourselves, with you;
And when distractions and thoughts rise up,
Which they will, help us with one sacred word
That is special to us, to come back to our intention
To be with you, to empty ourselves of the stuff that does not matter.
Help us simply to be still and know
That you are God, help us to be still,
To be.

Period of silence, after which say the Our Father from Matthew's Gospel, slowly and thoughtfully.

Our Father
Who art in heaven
Hallowed be thy name
Thy kingdom come
Thy will be done on earth
As it is in heaven.
Give us this day our daily bread
And forgive us our trespasses
As we forgive those who trespass against us
And lead us not into temptation
But deliver us from evil.
Amen

*See: Part III for more information on Centering Prayer
(the American spelling reflects the origin of this prayer method).

Prayer at the beginning of a school day (1)

Loving Father,
We gather at the beginning of a new school day
With all that is on our minds and in our hearts.
Help us to unwrap this new day as a gift from you
And give thanks for another opportunity to start again,
To live and learn. If yesterday wasn't so good, help us to do better.
If yesterday was awesome, help us with the one thing
That will make today even more awesome.

Help us with any worries we have right now –
Whether it's about school work, or a friendship, or something at home.
Help us to keep things in perspective,
To see the bigger picture.
We pray for those we love this morning,
For those who need our prayers,
For those who need our best attention.

Pause for silent intercession

Be with them, loving God,
And be with us on the journey of this day.
Inspire us to do all we can to make this school
A community of friendship, a place of peace,
Where everybody feels valued, safe and happy.
Help us to be cheerful and polite, to be kind to the people we meet
In the classroom, the corridor, the lunch queue, the playground.
Bless this day, bless this new beginning, and bless our school,
Through Christ our Lord, Amen.

Prayer at the beginning of a school day (II)

God of wisdom,
Help us to learn to speak and write well
So we can be advocates for change;
Help us to understand the importance of calculations
So we can build a better world;
Help us to grow healthy and strong
So we can help those who are in poor health;
Help us to appreciate beauty in art and music
So we can glimpse your presence in our world;
Help us to learn about other languages and cultures
So we can grow in respect for all our brothers and sisters;
Help us to learn about the story of God in Jesus
So we can tell others the Good News.

Prayer at the beginning of a school day for resilience

Loving God,
Give us resilience today –
In our lessons, on the sports field, in the playground
So that if something doesn't go well for us,
Or we get stuck in a lesson, or stumble on the sports field,
Our heads will not drop, we will not give in
But resolve that this is just something we can't do *yet*
And will apply ourselves to overcome
Our fear, our anxiety, and in turn
Help others who may be struggling;
In this way, we will learn the virtue of hope
And learn that the world will be made a better place
By people who do not give up at the first obstacle.

We make this prayer through Christ Our Lord.
Amen.

Did you Know?

According to UNESCO Institute of Statistics estimates, 24 million children will never enter a classroom. Half of all out-of-school children in sub-Saharan Africa will never enrol. Girls are the most disadvantaged, particularly in South and West Asia, where 80 per cent of out-of-school girls are unlikely to start school, compared to just 16 per cent for boys. UNESCO, UIS: Out of School Children Data Release 2015: http://goo.gl/nsrZ54

Teachers, if you get the chance, why not engage your class/form in some discussion about those statistics? Why might it be a problem that so many young people are not receiving an education, why is there such an imbalance in some parts of the world between boys and girls, why is education important in the first place?

Grace before meals

Bless us, O Lord,
And the food we are about to receive
Out of the goodness of the earth,
Our common home, which you bless with fruitfulness.

Bless those who do not have
The supply of food we take for granted.
May we never forget their needs
And do what we can to help.

May we eat our meal
With good manners, in the company of good friends
And remember to say "thank you"
To those who made it possible.

May we finish what is put before us,
Mindful that so much food in our world is wasted,
May we tidy up after ourselves
And use our energy well for the rest of the day.

We make this prayer through Christ our Lord.
Amen.

Tips for teachers

There are many ways to say grace before meals. Why not ask your class or form group to write their own grace before meals and then you'll have a ready supply to use every day before lunchtime in school? You could also ask the pupils to do some research and find some of the many forms of this important prayer.

Did you know?

Roughly one third of the food produced in the world for human consumption every year — approximately 1.3 billion tonnes — gets lost or wasted. Food losses and waste amounts to roughly US$ 680 billion in industrialized countries and US$ 310 billion in developing countries.

Source: Food and Agriculture Organization at the United Nations: http://www.fao.org/save-food/resources/keyfindings/en/, accessed 27 May 2017

Prayer at the end of a school day

God of all knowledge,
We give thanks for this day in school,
Another day to learn more about the wonders of your world
And to grow in the skills and understanding which will help us
To make the world a more just and compassionate place.

Help us to reflect honestly on those moments
When we were less than our best selves, when a thoughtless word
May have hurt someone, and sent them home this evening sad.
Help us tomorrow to be more thoughtful.

As we head home, may we remember that we are ambassadors
For our school and all it stands for.
On the bus or the train, help us to be thoughtful and polite,
To give up a seat for those who need it more than us.

And when we get home, let us remember
That our parents or carers have had a long day too.
May we be helpful around the house, take care with our homework
And turn off the phone long before bedtime!

On a birthday

Dear Father
Today it's *name* birthday –
We pray for your blessing on them
On their very special day.
Bless them today and all the days
Of their life; may they know
The kind of person you are calling them to be
In their one precious life;
Bless their family and friends
And everything they hold dear,
Protect them from harm and anxiety
And may they flourish on life's journey.
Help us to remember that their very presence here
Is a gift to our community.
May we always value them
And look out for them.
May they always remember
Their divine origin and eternal destiny,
That they are loved by you
More than they will ever realise
And that you know them
In the very depths of their heart.
We pray now in silence for them
And their intentions.

Pause for prayer of silent intercession.

We make our prayer for *name* today
Through Christ our Lord.
Amen.

If the class is in good voice
you may now wish to sing Happy Birthday!

Before a meeting

Loving Father
As we begin our meeting, help us to remember
The mission of our school: to make known to the world
Your plan for humankind, to live in unity and justice,
With particular regard for the lost and the least,
The victims of this world.

In all our decision-making,
May your Holy Spirit guide our thinking
So that we do not stray far from our purpose.
Help us at this meeting to play our part
In making our school a place where all can flourish,
Where studies are held to be important in so far
As they inspire our pupils to be agents of change,
Where in everybody we recognise your image and likeness,
Where we recognise and nourish the gift
That is every individual in this community.

In our meeting,
May all voices be heard with courtesy
May all show respect for each other
And may the end result be another small step
Towards the building up of your kingdom.
We ask this through Christ our Lord.
Amen.

Friday morning

Dear Lord,
Another week in school is almost over.
We look forward to the weekend and time
To be with our families, time to rest, to enjoy sport,
To hang out with friends, to go shopping, to catch up with homework;
To listen to what you are saying to us in the events of our life,
Reflecting on the questions which will help us to grow –

When did I feel your presence this week?
Did any mood or emotion this week take me by surprise?
What do I feel grateful for this week?
What am I sorry for this week?
Who do I need to make up with?
What line or phrase from the prayers or assembly stayed with me?

Dear Lord,
In this world of confusing signals
Help me to tune in to you, to listen
To the message of life; help me
To grow and mature into the person
You want me to be.

Tips for teachers

Whoever is leading the morning prayer, should read the questions very slowly, pausing in between each one. Encourage the pupils to be silent and reflective, with eyes closed perhaps. If the pupils use a prayer journal or equivalent, this is a good opportunity to answer some of the questions in writing and build up reflections and insights over time, developing the habit of reflection, writing down helpful phrases from prayers, assemblies or scripture.

In praise of creation

Feast of St Francis of Assisi, 4 October

For the radiant sun and brilliant moon,
For the galaxies and distant stars
For the unknown spaces of the universe.
R. Creator God, we praise you.

For the multitudinous oceans
For the broad rivers and humble streams
For the cooling breeze and driving rain.
R. Creator God, we praise you.

For the rich earth and the desert plain
For the fruitful trees and plants
The delicate flowers, industrious bees.
R. Creator God, we praise you.

For the wild, beautiful animals
For our good and faithful pets
For our own healthy bodies.
R. Creator God, we praise you.

For those who tend and keep the earth
For those who forgive for love of you
For those who work for peace.
R. Creator God, we praise you.

Did you know?

Laudato Si' the title of Pope Francis' encyclical on care for the earth, our common home, is a phrase taken from the beginning of St Francis of Assisi's famous "Canticle of the Sun" and it means "Praise be to you." Why not find out more about St Francis and why he is associated with care of the earth?

Harvest prayer

Harvest fast day, first Friday in October

God of the harvest,
We thank you for the fruits of the earth,
We thank you for the hands that plant the crops
And tend the flocks,
For those who look to the heavens for rain.

We have lost touch with the soil,
With what it means to sow and reap,
To wait with patience for the rains and green shoots.
We often take for granted what is on our plate.
We see farm machinery in our country
And endless fields of wheat,
But we don't know the back-breaking labour
Of farming with basic tools, digging the earth
To turn over tired soil, scattering seed,
Harvesting carefully, struggling to get a decent price for the crop.

We know there is more than enough to go around.
We know that a scandalous amount is wasted.
We know that one billion children in the world live in poverty.
Help us never to be indifferent to the real, daily needs
Of our brothers and sisters on this earth.
Help us to understand what fair trade means
And support those who treat the farmers
With dignity and justice.

Help us to bear good fruit in our own lives,
What it means to reap what we sow.
Help us to grow in responsibility for what we do,
For our earth, our common home,
For our brothers and sisters
Who live in places where life is much harder.
Bless all those who sow and reap.
Bless the harvest of the earth.
Bless the harvest of our lives.

Tips for teachers

You will find a wealth of resources to support your Harvest Day activities and prayers on the CAFOD website at: Cafod.org.uk/Education/fastday. Harvest Fast Day is usually around the beginning of October.

On a mufti day – how do I look?

God our Father,
When your Son came to earth
He didn't place much emphasis on clothes
Or dressing up in the latest styles.
In fact, he told us not to worry about such things.
In Luke's Gospel, Jesus says:
"Do not worry about your life, what you will eat,
Or about your body, what you will wear.
For life is more than food, and the body more than clothing."
Yet we are obsessed with brand recognition,
With getting the latest look, the coolest label.

Today, when we are in school in our own clothes
To raise money for good causes and to think about those
Who have much less than we have,
Let us not worry about how we look –
It is not important. God is more interested in our hearts
Than our tops or trainers or accessories.
Such things do not define us, although they can limit us.
May we never look down on anyone
Because they are not wearing the latest style or must-have item,
May we have the courage to challenge anyone, politely,
Who makes unkind comments about what another pupil is wearing.
(And let us not give a hard time to the one who forgot
and came into school in uniform!).

Today is a good day to give thanks for what we've got,
To try and understand why the goods of the earth are spread so unfairly,
To try to understand that what we wear was made by somebody,
somewhere
And not always in good conditions, not always for a fair wage.
Help us to develop an informed conscience about all our choices
And above all help us to remember that what is most important
Is not how we look, but the contents
Of our hearts.

Meditation on a one pound coin

Good morning, I'm glad I could join you for your prayers.
Let me tell you about my life
And maybe it will help you to understand our world a bit better.

I was given once to somebody's friend, who was skint,
Dropped in a mufti day collection at school, but can't remember the charity;
Given to a homeless man, who really valued me, but didn't keep me long,
Rammed into a slot machine in the arcade, quick shift in a supermarket trolley,
Flicked up to decide who kicked off, who went first, who won.
I spent some time in a fountain, trying to bring good luck,
I was used once for the wrong thing, and she knew it wasn't right.

I lived down the side of a sofa, and was found with a yell of delight.
I slept snug for a while in a piggy bank, and saw the light of day and a smile.
We had a reunion at Poundland, that was a lot of fun.
I was thrown in anger at a football match (not my proudest moment).
I was somebody's last pound of the week, held in a shaking hand.
I was tossed into the basket in church, although he couldn't afford to.
I was a tip, but not enough.

And now I'm a prop at morning prayer,
My best gig ever.

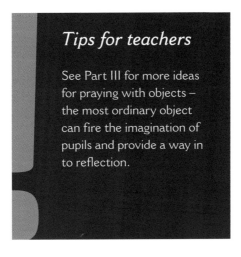

Tips for teachers

See Part III for more ideas
for praying with objects –
the most ordinary object
can fire the imagination of
pupils and provide a way in
to reflection.

Gratitude

God of all good things
Sometimes I complain about having a hard time
When things aren't going so well,
But help me to remember what I have to be grateful for,
Beginning with this morning –

I woke up in a warm bed,
My eyes opened and I could see.
I got out of bed unaided
And put on clean clothes.

I had a choice for breakfast,
And clean water to brush my teeth.
I had school books to put in my bag,
Someone to wave me off for the day,
A safe journey to school.

I have a school to go to,
I have teachers,
I have friends.

For all that and more
Thank you.

Did you know?

Eighty-five per cent of the world population lives in the driest half of the planet. Seven hundred and eighty-three million people do not have access to clean water and almost 2.5 billion do not have access to adequate sanitation. Six to eight million people die annually from the consequences of disasters and water related diseases.

Source: www.unwater.org > Water facts

All Saints

Holy day of Obligation, 1 November

God our Father,
Today we celebrate all the saints in heaven,
The communion of saints, the billions of souls
Thriving in your presence. The Church is so much bigger
And broader than we think, with the living
And the dead, the celebrity saints, the unknown saints,
The saints with the cool names like Agatha, Alphonsus, Aloysius, Ambrose,
Athanasius, Bede, Blaise, Barnabas, Bonaventure, Boniface, Clement,
Cyril, Cornelius, Edith, Fabian, Fidelis, Gertrude, Hedwig, Ignatius, Isidore,
Joachim, Justin, Maximilian, Norbert, Pancras, Perpetua, Polycarp,
Scholastica, Sixtus, Sylvester, Stanislaus, Titus;

And the names we know, names like our own, very much at home
With the all-stars of heaven, the team to be rooting for,
Except it's rooting for us, interceding for us
In the presence of God.
For every saint, there is a candle
So today we light a candle in our hearts for our saint,
The one who showed us a glimpse of God –
Our patron saint, our favourite saint, our school saint.
And we ask them to pray for us
Through Christ our Lord.
Amen.

Did you know?

When someone is made a saint by the Church, they are *canonised* by the pope.
The first papal canonisation took place in 993. Nowadays, canonisation is a lengthy
process. The Church has to make sure that the person being considered led an
exemplary life of holiness in service of God and others. There used to be a "devil's
advocate" who tried hard to find reasons why a candidate should *not* be canonised.
Before a canonisation can be approved it is necessary to confirm that two miracles
took place after intercession to the new saint. Most saints have their own feast days,
when they are commemorated.

All Souls

2 November

Loving Father,
We pray for all those we love
Who are no longer with us, who are now
In your merciful embrace. We pray for their eternal rest,
As the Church has done for hundreds of years.
We pray for those who are left behind,
Who feel the pain of loss, the sharp pangs
Of memory of time spent together.
We pray that we will be attentive
To those who mourn, who may need some help from us,
A loving word, a kind gesture.
Jesus in his earthly life knew the pain
Of losing a dear one: his father,
his friend and mentor, John the Baptist,
his friend Lazarus, whom he raised from the dead
but one day would die again.

Death is the part of life we struggle with.
In our society, it's not talked about much,
It's almost denied, since for many people
There is only this life, so the end of life
Is a disaster, a great loss, but that is not the faith
Of the Church: Jesus died and rose again, he conquered death.
Our friends and loved ones who have died
Have not disappeared; they live in the radiance of God,
Forgiven, loved, looked after.
This is our comfort, they are in better hands than ours.

For the fallen

Remembrance Day, 11 November

God of peace,
We pray for all victims of war,
We remember them, so that in remembering
Each new generation will know their sacrifice
And work even harder for peace.
We remember the lives lost in the mud and carnage
Of the First World War, and those who came home
Changed forever; we remember the great loss
Of the Second World War, brought home to our towns and cities
With bombs falling onto houses, factories and shipyards;
We remember the great effort to reclaim Europe from tyranny
And the campaigns in Africa and the Far East.
We remember the fallen of all wars since, sometimes very far from home,
And all civilians who have lost their lives.

We remember those who will not grow old,
As we that are left grow old, the young men who were called up
To serve their country and did not come home.
We remember those who came home bearing the scars of war,
Physical and psychological, for those today
Who need support to re-discover peace of mind and purpose.
We pray today, with all our hearts, for peace,
Pray that peace takes root
In the tender soil
Of our hearts.

Did you know?

According to Matthew White's estimate on the page *Worldwide Statistics of Casualties, Massacres, Disasters and Atrocities*, a total of about **123 million** people died in all wars of the twentieth century, comprising **37 million** military deaths, **27 million** collateral civilian deaths, **41 million** victims of "democide" (genocide and other mass murder) and **18 million** victims of non-democidal famine.

Source: necrometrics.com/all20c.htm

Anti-bullying week

November

God of Love,
We pray for those who sometimes bully others
In school, online, or to and from school.
Give them the grace to understand
The harm they are causing, to themselves as much as other people.
Give them the grace to break out of the cycle of bullying,
To see things from the point of view of those they hurt,
To have the courage to be reconciled,
To say sorry.

God of peace,
We pray for those who are sometimes bullied by others
In school, online, or to and from school.
Give them the grace to realise
That they are not alone
And to turn to their friends, family and teachers.
Give them the grace to break out of the cycle of bullying
By telling someone they trust what is going on
And to speak honestly about how they feel
So those who bully will learn and grow.

God of reconciliation,
Your Son revealed your nature to us,
He showed us that you are a gentle God
Who wills the good of all human beings,
Who wants to save us from the habits of sin.
Inspire us to follow the example of Jesus
And never lord it over others
Or use our power to make anyone feel bad about themselves
But to treat others the way Jesus treated them,
With dignity and compassion.

Tips for teachers

There are many excellent resources to support anti-bullying week and anti-bullying work throughout the year, such as Childline at https://www.childline.org.uk, or the Anti-Bullying Alliance at https://www.anti-bullyingalliance.org.uk/.

On friendship

We pray, dear Lord
For our friends and pray that we
Will be good friends in turn –
That we will be there when our friend needs us
And won't judge,
We will know when to say something
And when to say nothing;
We will be understanding when our friend is tired
And says something unkind
Or out of character;
We will forgive them when it's more than that;
We won't be possessive
When other friends come along;
We will find time
To be with our friend, in person,
And not just online;
We will give good advice
Even when we know it's not what
They want to hear;
We will tell the truth
Even at the risk of our friendship;
We will bring out the best
In our friend, help them to see their gifts
And help them to grow.

Dear Lord, you had good friends
And knew the good days and bad days,
Help me to understand
That real friendship is about giving
Without expecting anything
In return.

"If equal affection cannot be

Let the more loving one be me."

W. H. Auden,
"The More Loving One"

Christ the King

Final Sunday in Ordinary Time,
based on Matthew 25:31-46

Judge of the nations –

> *This is what you said would be our final judgement:*
> *What we did for the weak and vulnerable, the victims of our society,*

For the hungry –

> *whose crops have failed and go without food*
> *who go to Food Banks to feed their families*

For the thirsty –

> *whose water is unclean*
> *whose water sources are drying up due to human activity*

For the strangers –

> *who are new to our country and feel unwelcome*
> *who are lonely in our community*

For the naked –

> *who have been stripped of dignity by an uncaring world*
> *who have been humiliated online*

For the sick –

> *who suffer ill health with not enough medicine or help*
> *who suffer from anxiety or depression*

For the imprisoned –

> *who are trapped in debt or addiction*
> *who are in prison with little education or company*

Because whatever we do to them, we do it to you.

Advent: first week

God with us,
We begin the season of Advent,
The beginning of the Church's year,
With a wake-up call in the Gospel readings:
Be vigilant, get with it, get real.
Don't let your hearts get stuck in a rut,
Bogged down in the cares of life.
And what do we care about? Sometimes the wrong things,
Like how we look, or what we wear, or what phone
We've got. At this time of year, everything around us
Will remind us of what we want, but don't really need.
The high streets glitter with lovely stuff.

Help us to understand *gift* in a different way,
In a different currency, like time, or presence, or prayer,
And to think about giving more than receiving.
It's not easy, Lord, to swim against this tide.
The Gospel isn't telling us to be Scrooge,
But it is telling us to look at the condition of our hearts –
What treasure sits there?
The Gospel tells us that our liberation is at hand,
Liberation from the game of glamour, envy and greed.
So help us this advent, Lord,
To snap out of the dream of the world
And begin to look at things
With new eyes,
A new heart.

Did you know?

"The use of purple/violet in Advent suggests a state of unfulfilled readiness and should no longer be regarded as an expression of penitence. It serves to set off the joyful white of Christmas with greater dramatic effect."

Season of Advent, http://www.liturgyoffice.org.uk/Calendar/Seasons/Advent.pdf, accessed 10 July 2017.

Advent: second week

God of salvation,
All through the history of Israel
You sent prophets to show the people
The true path, the right way to behave,
Preparing them for the full revelation of your nature
In the person of Jesus, born in Bethlehem.
At this time of year, we hear about the prophet John the Baptist,
A voice crying in the wilderness, living a tough life
On a diet of locusts and wild honey,
Completely focused on his mission to prepare
A way for the Lord. His message was "repent"
And as we continue our Advent journey we reflect
On what we should be sorry for,
For those aspects of our life which we know are not quite right
And need to change, for those habits
Which do not serve you or our neighbour but only ourselves.

We also think of "repent" as an invitation to change,
To change our mindset,
To consider where we look for happiness.
Is it in loving relationships with people, giving our time
And talent to others,
Or in things which are passing and shallow?
Give us the grace, loving Father,
To repent, to change the way we see things,
Slowly but surely, until we see the world
Through the compassionate eyes
Of Jesus Christ, your Son,
Our Lord.

"A Europe-wide study of seasonal shopping has found that UK Christmas spending will lead the continent to hit a record £77.56bn in 2016. Although UK Christmas spending will only be up by 1.9 per cent year-on-year, UK households are set to spend almost double the European average. The UK Christmas spending bonanza will be powered along by mobile devices, which will experience a major growth of 51.2 per cent on 2015."

http://realbusiness.co.uk/sales-and-marketing/2016/11/24/uk-christmas-spending-hit-record-77-56bn-in-2016/, accessed 8 July 2017.

Advent: third week

God of wisdom,
Your prophet John the Baptist
Fired the imagination of the people –
They came from all over and made the hard journey
Into the wilderness to hear him.
There was a stir going on, they sensed something big,
An urgent message about the kingdom of God.
"What must we do?" they asked him, each in turn:
Tax collectors, soldiers, ordinary people.
His answers give us a glimpse of the message of Jesus:
Share what you've got with the needy, be honest, don't bully people.

John announced Good News to the poor
And we wonder what he meant by that.
There are still poor people in the world,
Many more, in fact, than at the time of Jesus.
There are those without enough food to eat,
Those who travel across oceans and continents
With their possessions in a plastic bag to seek safety,
Those who have no place to call home.
The Good News is that the poor have great dignity
In the eyes of God, they are loved
And we are called to love them, to make that love known.

But more than that, we will hear Jesus say
That you will find *him* in the poor,
In the least of these, his brothers and sisters.
The poor and vulnerable must no longer be treated badly, or exploited,
Not just because we should love them
But because we find in them
Our humble God.

Advent: fourth week

God of creation,
You chose a young woman in a Galilean village
To bear your Son into the world.
It is hard to imagine how Mary must have felt
When in the course of an ordinary day –
Kneading dough, drawing water, sweeping the floor –
An angel, no less, interrupted her with a troubling message:
She was going to conceive a child
Whom she would call Jesus and his kingdom would last forever.
Mary was perplexed by this, she wasn't even married,
So how could she conceive a son?
It shows great inner strength to come back to an angel with a question.
By the power of the Holy Spirit, answered the angel.

In some old paintings, all the angels of heaven
Looked on while Mary pondered this mission
Which will change her quiet life forever.
The great God of the universe needed the co-operation
Of this young woman to become a human being.
Mary had a choice, heaven for a moment held its breath
And when she said "let it be" a shout of joy echoed around the stars.
Mary would be the gateway, the perfect channel
For God the Father to become human
And tell humanity once and for all what he was like.
As we consider the conception of God
In the womb of the Virgin Mary,
We pray for all expectant mothers at this time,
We pray for the unborn,
We pray that everyone in our society
Will value the great gift
Of human life.

Nativity of the Lord

Holy day of obligation, 25 December

Dear God,
On this holy day
We remember the great mystery of the incarnation,
That you loved the world so much that you sent your Son
To be one of us, born not in a palace
Or even a comfortable home, but in the place
In the house where they kept the animals, downstairs,
In the muck and smell.
This humble beginning tells us
That you are not a God of power the way we think about power,
Not a God of show and pretence, but a quiet God
Who enters history with no ceremony.

There were a few visitors: in Luke's Gospel
The lowly ones, the shepherds, in Matthew's Gospel
The wise men with their gifts.
They can stand in for all of us, the human race
Gathered around the manger, with our hopes and fears,
With our heartfelt prayers for peace:
Peace in our hearts, in our homes, in the places on earth
Destroyed by war and violence.
As we kneel before the God of the universe
Held tightly in the arms of Mary, his mother and ours,
We pray for our fragile world,
That in this vulnerable child we will find our joy,
Our light in the darkness,
Our dignity as human beings,
Our common cause,
Our hope.

Did you know?

In the Church's year, the season of Christmas, or Christmas Time, runs from Evening Prayer on Christmas Eve, 24 December, up to and including the Sunday after Epiphany or after 6 January.

Epiphany of the Lord

Holy day of obligation, 6 January, except when this falls on a Saturday or a Monday when it is transferred to the adjacent Sunday

Loving Father, in the Epiphany
Your love was revealed to us in the form of a child.
As we kneel before the holy infant with the wise men, and adore

We offer the gold of our hearts, what is best in us;
We offer the frankincense of our prayers, a sweet aroma;
We offer the oil of myrrh as our commitment to the end.

We ask for a blessing on our homes and our school
Which we mark with the letters C + M + B and the year of the Lord.
Christus Mansionem Benedicat. May Christ bless this house!

Bless all those in our school who came from afar
To join our community; bless their families.
May all be at home in the presence of the Christ child.

Holocaust Memorial Day

27 January, http://hmd.org.uk/

One day
In a concentration camp
Two men and a boy
Were sentenced to execution
By hanging.

The men died quickly.
The boy, lighter, took longer.
The prisoners were made to watch.
A voice cried out,
"Where is God?"

Then there was silence.
Did God die
In the concentration camps?
Is it possible to pray
After such horror?

We pray now
Because some prayed *in* the camps,
In the deepest darkness.
We cry out,
"Where was humanity?"

We commit ourselves
To remember
That six million Jews
And others the Nazi regime
Labelled expendable

Were gassed to death
With cyanide,
Their dead bodies burned in furnaces,
Their ashes carried
On the wind.

We are not innocent:
For many centuries
Christians were hostile to Jewish people,
Persecuted them
For the death of Jesus.

The Holocaust took place
Within living memory,
In one of the most educated
And Christian countries
In history.

We beg forgiveness
For the crimes against the Jewish people,
Against humanity,
And pray for the grace
To be vigilant,

To stand up
Against anti-Semitism and racism
In any shape or form
We may encounter it
In our world today.

"Then came the march past the victims. The two men were no longer alive. Their tongues were hanging out, swollen and bluish. But the third rope was still moving: the child, too light, was still breathing...

And so he remained for more than half an hour, lingering between life and death, writhing before our eyes. And we were forced to look at him at close range. He was still alive when I passed him. His tongue was still red, his eyes not yet extinguished.

Behind me, I heard the same man asking: 'For God's sake, where is God?'

And from within me I heard a voice answer: 'Where is He? This is where - hanging from this gallows...'

That night, the soup tasted of corpses."

Elie Wiesel, *Night*
(London: Penguin Books, 2008)

"The religious interest of the prisoners, as far and as soon as it developed, was the most sincere imaginable. The depth and vigour of religious belief often surprised and moved a new arrival. Most impressive in this connection were the improvised prayers or services in the corner of a hut, or in the darkness of the locked cattle truck in which we were brought from a distant work site, tired, hungry and frozen in our ragged clothing."

Viktor E. Frankl, *Man's Search for Meaning*
(London: Random House, 2004)

"In her rejection of every persecution against any man, the Church, mindful of the patrimony she shares with the Jews and moved not by political reasons but by the Gospel's spiritual love, decries hatred, persecutions, displays of anti-Semitism, directed against Jews at any time and by anyone."

Second Vatican Council, *Nostra Aetate*
(Declaration on the Relation of the Church to Non-Christian Religions), 4

Martin Luther King Day

Martin Luther King Day is a federal holiday in America,
celebrated annually on the third Monday in January

God of peace,
Over the years you sent us prophets
To cry out against injustice
And to speak truth to power,
Prophets like Martin Luther King
Who stood up to racial segregation and injustice
In America, who had a dream
Of children of different races and backgrounds living in harmony,
Of a society where the content of a person's character
Was considered more important
Than the colour of their skin,
Who insisted on nonviolence as the way to make that dream a reality,
Who paid for that dream with his life.
Give us the strength of Martin Luther King
To stand up to racism
In any shape or form we encounter it,
Which is sometimes blatant,
But sometimes subtle.
May we never be fooled and never let it pass,
We make this prayer
Through Christ our Lord.
Amen.

"The Church reproves, as foreign to the mind of Christ, any
discrimination against men or harassment of them because of their
race, colour, condition of life, or religion."

Second Vatican Council, *Nostra Aetate*
(Declaration on the Relation of the Church to Non-Christian Religions), 5

Safer internet day

https://www.saferinternet.org.uk/safer-internet-day

Creator God,
We thank you for technology,
For the brilliant minds of men and women
Who have given us such advances,
The awesome power of a cell phone
With more computational capacity
Than the computer that put a man on the moon.
So much good has come of this technology,
People in contact with friends and loved ones far away,
An entire library in the palm of our hands,
The sum of human knowledge in our pocket.

Lord, we also know the damage
That this technology can cause in the wrong hands
With those who seek to steal the identity of others
Or lead young people into harm,
Or who abuse others online as a kind of sport.
May we always consider thoughtfully what we say
And what we post online.
May we always remember
That it is a person who receives and reads our messages
And the smallest comment or emoji
Can hurt someone.

Help us to remember that knowledge
Is not the same as wisdom
And that virtual reality
Is not a place where friendships flourish:
True friendship deepens
In the real presence of another
And a true friend knows that.

For the sick

World Day for the Sick, 11 February,
Feast of Our Lady of Lourdes

Healing Lord,
We pray for all those who are sick today,
Especially those with no-one to care for them
Or tell them they are loved.
We pray for all our friends and family
Who are ill at this time.

Pause for silent intercession

We do not know if our prayers
Will heal them, that is in your hands.
What we ask for is that we will be more attentive
To their needs, to see life from their point of view,
To give them our time in a visit,
To think carefully
About what would make them feel better.

Loving Father,
We place those who are sick
In your care, in the arms of Mary,
Our loving mother.

Lent: Ash Wednesday

Today, ashes
Are thumbed onto our forehead
As a sign that we are human,
Fragile, and will sometimes
Get it wrong.

They are also an invitation
To turn away from sin
And believe in the Gospel,
The Good News of Jesus Christ
Who loved us to the end.

Ash Wednesday
Begins the season of Lent,
Forty days of reflection and action: prayer,
Fasting from what's not good for us
And almsgiving.

The colour is violet.
The volume is turned down,
The Alleluia is put away in its box,
The Gloria is unplugged.
Time to go deeper.

We pray, and fast
And give alms to the needy
So that we can come closer to God and our neighbour,
To the presence of love
That is never far from us.

Dear Lord,
May we be open this Lent
To your love, so that we may know
We are reconciled to you,
That we are friends.

Did you know?

"In the Roman rite, the beginning of the forty days of penance is marked with the austere symbol of ashes which are used in the Liturgy of Ash Wednesday. The use of ashes is a survival from an ancient rite according to which converted sinners submitted themselves to canonical penance. The act of putting on ashes symbolizes fragility and mortality and the need to be redeemed by the mercy of God."

http://www.liturgyoffice.org.uk/Calendar/Seasons/Lent.pdf, accessed 12 July 2017

Lent begins on Ash Wednesday and lasts until just before the Mass of the Lord's Supper on Holy Thursday. We then have three special days, the *Easter Triduum*, which will help us prepare for the great joy of Easter morning, the resurrection of Jesus.

Lent: Tempted

Before he went public
With the Good News
That the kingdom of God
Was at hand,
Jesus faced his temptations.

He was tempted
To turn stones into bread,
To enjoy physical pleasures
As if they mattered more
Than the word of God.

He was tempted
To throw himself from a height,
To test the love of his Father
Rather than just trusting
Like everybody else.

He was tempted
To use his charisma
To gain power in this world.
If he abandoned God
It would all be his.

God of the wilderness,
We are tempted too, every day,
To walk an easier path,
To put the pleasures of this world
Before following you.

Give us the grace this Lent,
In our wilderness of reflection,
To resist the temptations, to fast from one thing
That will bring us closer to you
And our neighbour.

Did you know?

"The use of violet or purple vestments and the simplicity of decoration in the church reflect the penitential nature of the season."

http://www.liturgyoffice.org.uk/Calendar/Seasons/Lent.pdf, accessed 12 July 2017

Lent: Transfigured

One day
Jesus went up a mountain
With his closest friends –
Peter, James and John – to pray.
Like a Lent retreat.

A question
Had been on his mind:
"Who do people say I am?"
The answers were confusing:
John the Baptist, Elijah.

In his prayer
He got an answer
That made his face radiant:
"This is my Son, the chosen one."
He knew he was loved.

It is love
Which transfigures us,
Makes us shine,
Just as lack of love disfigures,
Keeps us in the dark.

It can take a long time
For us to learn that.
Even the disciples, who were with Jesus,
Didn't always understand
What was going on.

Father of love,
As we walk up our mountain this Lent
Help us in our prayers,
In the silence of our hearts,
To know we are loved.

Lent: Living water

One day, at noon,
Jesus met a woman by a well.
She was drawing water
On her own, an outcast in the village.
He was tired and thirsty.

"Give me water," he said.
They should not even have spoken,
According to the custom.
He was a Jew, she was a Samaritan.
She had a reputation.

But Jesus spoke to her,
The first gentle voice she'd heard for a while,
And did not judge her past
Or her present.
He looked into her soul

And she felt so loved
And redeemed
That she left her jar by the well
And ran into the village
To tell them about this prophet.

Jesus wants our company
By the well, the places we stop
For rest and refreshment.
We have nothing to prove,
He knows us better than anyone.

God of life,
Bring us to the living water
Of your presence, where we are not judged
But accepted and loved
Just as we are.

Lent: The blind man

Disability
In the ancient world
Was thought to be a punishment
For the sins of your parents.
Jesus did not agree.

When he met a blind man
His disciples asked if his parents had sinned.
Jesus said no – his blindness
Was so that the works of God
Might be displayed in him

And he made a paste,
Put it on the man's eyes
And restored his sight,
Much to the anger of the Pharisees:
It was a Sabbath day.

Are we blind
To the disability around us?
We may not see it as punishment
(although some still do)
But what do we 'see' –

Do we see the world
From the point of view
Of someone with visual impairment,
Or a wheelchair user,
Or someone with a complete lack of mobility?

Lord, help us to know
Our blind spots, help us to see
With the eyes of compassion
So that we become more aware
Of the needs of others.

Lent: Lazarus

Jesus wept
When he heard the news
Of the death of his friend Lazarus.
He felt the depths of human emotions
Like we do.

When he'd heard Lazarus was very ill,
He did not rush to be with him
And his sisters Martha and Mary.
He waited, as if he knew
That the power of God would be displayed.

But still he wept
And sighed from the heart
When he met his grieving friends.
He told them to roll away the stone.
Everyone watched in awe

As the shadow of Lazarus
Appeared at the mouth of the tomb.
He was still wrapped in grave-clothes:
"Unbind him," said Jesus,
"Let him go free."

Almighty Father,
What is dead in us
That needs to be unbound?
Our love for those
Who brought us into the world?

Our sense of wonder?
Our imagination, our kindness?
Time can blunt our best instincts,
Make us careless and cold.
Help our best selves to rise again.

Lent: Palm Sunday

At the beginning
Of his final week on earth, Holy Week,
Jesus entered Jerusalem
Not as a military hero, on a horse,
But on a donkey.

The people expected
A messiah to liberate them
From Roman occupation,
To bring home the scattered tribes,
Restore the temple.

The vision of Jesus
For a new Israel was different –
No distinction between people,
No displays of military power,
No patriotic speeches.

The kingdom of God
Would be universal forgiveness,
Looking at relationships in a new way,
Not as power or payback
But as love.

Jesus is forever
Coming into our world
On a donkey,
On a leaking dinghy,
In the back of a lorry.

We've looked for him
Often in the wrong places,
In magnificent buildings, in powerful people.
Lord, help us to see you
In the humble.

A liturgy of stones

Examination of conscience

Imagine you are holding a stone in your hand.
Imagine that this stone is the one thing lodged in your heart
That holds you back from being a better person: more open, more giving.

It could be your pride, your burnished ego,
Your need to put people down, or say the wrong thing,
Your coldness in the face of need.

What resides in the heart of your stone?
Close your hand over it
And take it into your heart, admit its presence.

Pause for reflection (with music if available)

Open your hand and your heart.
Consider again your stone, made smooth over countless years
By the patience of tides and sand.

In the same way, God works on your soul,
Like a potter with clay, shaping you, forming you,
Willing you to be the person he intended you to be.

All that is asked of you is to be open to grace,
To the life of God which is never far from any of us,
Be open and trusting like a child.

Now take your stone, with what it represents
And leave it at the foot of the cross
Where Jesus took on all our sins, all our stones.

On the third day, the power of God
Shattered the stone, transformed the broken body
And proclaimed in the Risen One forgiveness and peace.

Easter Triduum: Holy Thursday

On the night before he died, Jesus had a last supper with his friends
And showed them how to remember forever
What his mission was all about, what they were supposed to do.

He got a basin of water and got down on his knees
To wash their feet, one at a time. This was just not done.
There were servants in those days to wash the dusty feet of guests.

Peter spoke up, unhappy about this, but Jesus told him
This was the way: serve each other in humility, serve the poor.
This is what he meant when he gave us his body.

Lord, help us to grow in the ministry of service,
To understand that the purpose of life is not to gain power
Possessions and prestige, but simply to serve.

Easter Triduum: Good Friday

Because what he said and did was such a threat to the ways
Of the religious authorities, they made sure he was condemned
And flogged and taken out and nailed up onto a cross.

The disciples could not cope with the violence, the crowds –
Only his mother and the women stayed, and the beloved disciple.
Roman crucifixion was a humiliation, a public mockery.

Jesus became human and went to the very depths of being human –
Abandoned by God, tortured, and made a victim.
He did not fight back, he absorbed the violence of the human race

And from his high place on the cross, outside the walls of the city, forgave us.
Lord, we do not know what we are doing, help us
To forgive and be reconciled, never again to make victims.

Easter Triduum: Resurrection

The rock split and a shaft of light shone into the darkness.
Only the angels witnessed the resurrection,
The power of the Spirit transforming Jesus into glory.

Mary Magdalen was the first to know, arriving early to find
The empty tomb, called to a new life when she heard her name
Spoken by the risen Lord, whose very breath

Was peace. There was no revenge, now he was risen,
No lessons in power for those men who struck him
And flogged him. That's what we would do.

He simply forgave, and taught his friends the meaning of everything
He had said and done, and told them to wait
Until the Spirit powered them up to go out and tell the world:

Christ is Risen, his light spreads over all the earth.

He has forgiven every one of our sins and shown us the path to God.

Plug in the Gloria, sing alleluia, praise the Lord.

Did you know?

The season of Easter, or Easter Time, is the fifty days from
Easter Sunday to Pentecost. They are celebrated as one feast
day, sometimes called "the Great Sunday". The singing of the
alleluia is characteristic of these days. The Ascension is
celebrated on the fortieth day after Easter and Pentecost
fifty days after Easter. The liturgical colour of Easter is white.

The Ascension

Holy day of obligation, to be celebrated
on Thursday in the sixth week of Easter

If you have ever lost someone very dear to you,
Have you noticed how they are still present
In your memory, in your heart?
It's as if when their body has gone
Their spirit is still with you
And you get to know them in a different way –
You might say you're in contact with the essence
Of who they were as a person
And now you get to know them almost in a deeper way
Than when they were with you,
Without the ups and downs, good days and bad days
Of being with them in person.
Of course, we still want them with us,
But separation, at least in the body, is sadly part of life.
When Mary Magdalen met the risen Jesus on Easter Sunday morning
He said something strange to her,
It sounded almost cold – "Do not cling to me," he said.
Maybe the message here is that Jesus of Nazareth
Could only have been with us for a short time.
He had to return to the Father, as we all do,
But the Good News is that we have his Spirit still with us,
Which is like a bigger presence than any one human life can contain.

Lord, as we contemplate your ascension
Back to the Father, help us to understand
That you never left us, your Spirit is still with us.
May we take comfort and strength from your last words to the disciples
At the end of Matthew's Gospel:
"I am with you always, to the end of time."

Did you know?

Christ is present not just in his Spirit. The Fathers of the Second Vatican Council reminded us that Christ is present in the Mass and in his word, the scriptures. He is also present, "when the Church prays and sings", for he promised: "Where two or three are gathered together in my name, there am I in the midst of them" (Matthew 18:20). *Sacrosanctum Concilium*, (the Constitution on the Sacred Liturgy), paragraph 7. This means that when you pray as a class, or form group, Christ is present.

Pentecost

Fifty days after the resurrection

God of inspiration,
After Jesus your Son had returned to you
The disciples huddled together in an upper room,
With Mary and the family of Jesus, and the women
Who stood at the foot of the cross.

They felt the absence of their Lord
Who for a few precious days after his resurrection
Had appeared to them, walked with them, ate with them,
Taught them what the scriptures meant, breathed peace on them.
For the two sad friends on the road to Emmaus
Whose hopes had been crushed by the death of Jesus
There was recognition of him at the breaking of the bread.
With hearts on fire they rushed back to tell the others.

But now they were alone.
What should they do without the loving presence of their Lord?
Jesus had told them to wait and not to worry, he promised
He would send them his Spirit. So they waited. And waited.

Until out of nowhere, a rush of wind filled the house.
It blew open the shutters, blew open their hearts,
Filled the whole house, filled the rest of their lives.
Then a strange and wonderful sight: fire, which did not burn them,
Divided into smaller tongues of flame and rested on each of them.
The Holy Spirit, the Spirit of Jesus, Spirit of the living God:
Filled them, blessed them, inspired them
And set them off on travels round the whole known world
To proclaim the Good News of Jesus Christ, to found his Church,
To build his kingdom of peace and reconciliation
And show the way to you, loving Father, the source of love and grace.

*

Two thousand years later,
We don't expect the windows to blow in,
But we pray for the same Spirit to flood our hearts.
We pray for the gifts of the Spirit:
For wisdom in the flow of endless data
For understanding among the shallow soundbites
For good choices in the face of bad advice
For strength to stay the course and do the right thing
For true knowledge in an age of fake news
For holiness when the holy is not believed in
For wonder before the marvels of God.

Did you know?

As well as the gifts of the Spirit, the Church teaches that those who are open to the Spirit will bear the fruits of the Spirit, which St Paul lists as: "love, joy, peace, patience, kindness, generosity, faithfulness, gentleness and self-control" (Galatians 5:22-23).

St Joseph

St Joseph has two feast days in the liturgical calendar.
The first is 19 March: Joseph, the Husband of Mary;
the second is 1 May: Joseph, the Worker.

Worker in wood and stone, skilled with hammer and chisel,
Man of courage who protected Mary from the demands of the law
That someone in her position should be stoned.
You made a home for her and the unborn Son of God.

We do not know when you died, or how many years
You had with Mary and Jesus in the dusty little village of Nazareth.
We don't know if you took Jesus with you to that job in Sepphoris
Where Herod was rebuilding the town –

A new theatre and colonnades, new houses,
Lots of work and a good place to learn a trade,
See something of the world, learn a bit of Greek.
Who knows? You passed quietly out of history, unnoticed.

Joseph the worker, husband, father –
Pray for the workers, that they may have dignity,
Pray for the husbands, that they may be loving,
Pray for the fathers, that they may be patient and wise.

A prayer for the hands

God of created things,
Your Son worked with his hands,
Apprenticed to his human father Joseph

He learned to work in wood and stone,
shaping and measuring, sawing and chiselling,
getting the line just right, the fit snug.

Bless the hands we take for granted,
The hands that help us on our way, that provide for us,
That pick us up when we stumble.

Bless the hands that combed and brushed our hair
When we were younger, and maybe still do,
The hands that held ours when we could not be trusted on the road.

Bless the hands that serve our food,
The hands that planted and raised the crops
That made it all the way to our plate.

Bless the hands that stitched and sewed our clothes,
That pinned and packed our shirts and tops, sometimes
For less than we would call a living wage.

Bless the hands that fix our bodies when they're broken,
Remove malignity, sew up wounds,
Take our temperature, tell us when to slow down.

Bless the hands that mark our books,
That help us grow in skill and understanding,
That point us on the way to truth.

Bless the hands that bless us,
No matter what we've done, the hands
that bless us anyway.

Vocation – what is my path?

Luke 12:13-21, The Parable of the Rich Fool

Heavenly Father
Help us today to reflect on our path in life –
We do not know what the future holds
Or what we will be doing in ten, twenty, thirty years' time.
We know that in previous generations
People stayed in the same job very often
For their entire lives: forty years
As a teacher, nurse, salesman, docker, then retirement.
We know it's not like that now,
We may have five or six different jobs before we're thirty
And we may struggle to get the right job for us,
Or get any job at all.
Help us to prepare well for life in modern Britain,
To develop the "soft skills" which are important today:
To communicate well, to solve problems, to get on with different people;
To develop the qualities which will help us contribute to society:
Openness, respect for others, reliability;
To develop the values that will help us build the kingdom:
Compassion, humility, integrity, simplicity, love.
Guide us on the next steps in our path through life,
Help us to listen to your voice
Prompting us to go where we can make the best difference,
Where our unique blend of skills and qualities
Can serve others. We will hear messages
That life is about making money, building bigger barns,
Being a success in our chosen field.
That's not what we find in the Gospel.
Help us to understand our true path, to become the persons
You want us to be, to have the courage
To swim against the tide if needs be
And not to become too anxious about the future
But to trust in your plans for us.

Mary, Mother of God

May is the month of Mary

Hail Mary, most highly favoured lady,
Mother of God, who conceived God in her womb
By the power of the Holy Spirit,
Pray for us in this valley of history –
A valley of tears, a valley of joy, a valley of fear, a valley of hope.

We make our way on this long and winding road,
Sometimes with a light step, sometimes with a heavy heart,
Doing our best to make the most of what comes our way.
It's not always easy, dear Mother, as you know –
You pondered many things in the depth of your blessed heart.

In this month of May, your month,
A month of apple blossom and lighter days,
Pray for us your children, pray for us
At the two most important moments in our life: now
And at the hour of our death.

Amen

Did you know?

At the Council of Ephesus in AD 431, in modern day Turkey, Mary was declared *Theotokos*, meaning Mother of God or God Bearer. It is said that the people of the city took to the streets with torches in celebration when they heard the announcement. The term *Theotokos* had been in use for many years before the Council's official endorsement. Mary had a very special place in the hearts of Christians from the beginning. In the Catholic tradition, we pray to Mary to intercede for us with her Son, we do not worship Mary. The most popular devotion associated with Mary is the rosary, a rich spiritual exercise. Why not ask the pupils to do some research into the feast days of Mary and the apparitions at Lourdes and Fatima, which are a great source of grace for many people?

Litany to Mary, Mother of God

The response (R.) after each line is "Pray for us"

Mary, whose world was turned upside down by an angel – R.
Mary, who said yes to God – R.
Mary, who gave birth in poverty – R.

Mother of a family who fled violence – R.
Mother of a boy who went missing – R.
Mother of a young man who left home to follow a dream – R.

Mother of a man the community rejected – R.
Mother of a teacher who inspired love and suspicion – R.
Mother of a son was who was held up for ridicule – R.

Mother who saw her son die – R.
Mother who saw her son rise – R.
Mother who pondered all this in her heart – R.

Mary, comfort of the afflicted – R.
Mary, queen of peace – R.
Mary, morning star – R.

Mary, Mother of the Church, our Mother in heaven – R.

Blessed be God, three in one

Inspired by St Paul's second letter to the Corinthians 1:1-7

Blessed be God the Father, origin of life and love,
A gentle Father and the God of all consolation,
Who comforts us in all our sorrows,
So that we can offer others, in their sorrows,
The consolation that we have received from God.

Blessed be Jesus Christ, God in human form,
One of us, who knew the satisfaction of a day's hard work,
Who knew the joy of sunrise over the lake, breakfast with friends,
The pain of betrayal, the fear of the mob –
Redeemer, teacher, friend.

Blessed be the Holy Spirit, breath of God,
Life of God, inspiration of the whole human race –
Our best ideas, our unexplained moments of goodness,
A sudden shaft of light,
Our humble guide on the path of life.

In the wilderness

Corpus Christi, The Most Holy Body and Blood of Christ,
Holy day of obligation, Thursday after Trinity Sunday,
or the following Sunday

Inspired by Deuteronomy 8:2-3, 14-16
Lord our God,
You led the people of Israel
Into the wilderness for forty years
To test them, humble them
And help them to get to know
Their inmost heart.
Help us to remember that when we feel
That we are in our own "wilderness" –
Not really sure what's going on,
Where we're going
Or who we are.

In the wilderness
You fed the people of Israel
With manna from heaven.
In John's Gospel
Jesus told the crowd
That he was the living bread come down from heaven –
Food for the soul, for eternal life.
May we never lose heart
In our wilderness moments
But remember
That you will nourish us
And keep us safe on our journey.

Before the Blessed Sacrament

As we gather together in sacred time
Help us to be still, to gradually set aside
What's on our mind,
The worries that work away at us,
And be really present in the real presence of the risen Christ,
To rest in this moment of grace
Where time meets eternity,
Where the material world shines with the presence of God
And know that we are loved.
We have nothing to prove in the presence of the living God,
No deadlines to meet, no goals to reach.
We are not being tested.
God only wants us, plain simple us, the us
We often hide from the world, even from our friends,
Because we're afraid it might not be good enough.
God does not love us because we're good
But we are good because he loves us
And he wants us to be open to that love, trusting
In his plans for us.

Lord Jesus Christ, present before us,
Help us also to see your presence in our neighbour,
In the pupils and staff around us,
In the weak and vulnerable of the world,
In your blessed creation,
In ourselves –
If only we could believe
That such a treasure is so close.

Tips for teachers

Another popular devotional practice is Adoration of the Blessed Sacrament, when individuals spend time in prayer before the real presence of the risen Christ in the host consecrated at Mass. The host is presented in a monstrance. Adoration often ends with Benediction (or blessing) of the Blessed Sacrament. This traditional practice is enjoying a revival in many parishes and schools. The theology of the real presence may at first be an obstacle to staff and pupils with no religious background. Before embarking on any explanation of this, it would be advisable to consult with the school's chaplain, head of RE, headteacher, or the diocese. In essence, the message to the pupils is that they are in the presence of God. Adoration of the Blessed Sacrament is an occasion of grace and peace. It will generally take place in school with larger gatherings, perhaps a year group, or will be available throughout the day for pupils and staff to make visits.

For peace of mind

Mental Health Awareness Week,
see https://www.mentalhealth.org.uk/get-involved

God of compassion,
Today we pray for all those in our world
Who suffer from poor mental health,
Whose minds are in turmoil,
Whose daily routines are an agony of confusion
Doubt and darkness.

The young in our society
Face mental ill health due to anxiety
About their bodies, their weight, their looks,
Anxiety about school and exams,
Friendships and family.

The solutions seem easy enough –
Sleep well, eat well, go for long walks,
Talk about your feelings,
Get a hobby. We know that's true,
But easier said than done.

We know that your Son,
While on earth, suffered anxiety,
The ultimate anxiety of knowing that death,
Violent death, was imminent
And his Father seemed to have abandoned him.

Jesus knew that we were worriers
And tried to calm our souls. In Matthew's Gospel he said:
"I am telling you not to worry about your life
And what you are to eat, nor about your body
And how are to clothe it."

He knew that we carried burdens:
Some guilt we can't shake off,
A relationship that's stuck in a rut,
A low sense of our own worth,
A family tradition we can't live up to.

So he said to the crowds:
"Come to me, all you who labour
And are overburdened, and I will give you rest.
Shoulder my yolk and learn from me
For I am gentle and humble in heart
And you will find rest for your souls."

For freedom from anxiety

A collect*

Loving Father

Who formed us in our mother's womb
And knows us better than we know ourselves

Free us from the anxieties
That prevent us from being the person you want us to be

So that we may live fruitful
And fulfilled lives in your service

We make this prayer through Christ our Lord, your Son,
Who knew the fragile depths of the human heart.
Amen.

*See: Part III for more information on the collect
as a prayer form.

Who am I?

Who do you think you are?
Is the phrase used for the upstart,
The one who has gotten above himself, herself,
Who has climbed out of someone else's definition,
And those who define and confine
Don't like it, hence the need
To put them "back in their box"
Where they belong.

Lord, you knew the process
Of human self-discovery,
Finding out who you were
In a small community
Who didn't like it when one day
You spoke to them as a prophet
When they knew you as Joseph's son, the builder,
And that's where they wanted you to stay,
Safe in that definition.

Today there are many people
Who would define us
According to our age, race, gender, neighbourhood
And want to keep us there,
In our place.

There are many people
Who put too many choices in front of us,
Too many options on Facebook.
Sometimes I wonder
Who am I?

Help me to remember
That in the eyes of God I am
Blessed
Forgiven
Gifted
Loved

Every hair on my head has been counted.

Prayer for life

Day for Life is the day in the Church's year dedicated to raising awareness about the meaning and value of human life at every stage and in every condition. The Church teaches that life is to be nurtured from conception to natural death. To find out the date of the next Day for Life, please visit http://www.dayforlife.org/

God of life,
We pray for the unborn,
Who should be safe
In their mother's womb,
The place where you form them in love
And know them.

We pray for all mothers
Who are tempted
To abort their unborn child
For convenience, or out of shame;
Grant them the vision
Of the life they carry.

God of life,
We pray for the elderly,
Who should be safe
In their infirmity, at home
Or in the care of loving hands.
Grant them peace in old age.

We pray for the terminally ill
And those who care for them,
That despite their distress
They will not be tempted to end life;
Grant them the grace
To see life through to its natural end.

We pray for all legislators
Who in many places
Allow the unborn and elderly or ill to be killed;
Grant them the grace
Of understanding how precious
Each life is in your eyes.

"You knit me together in my mother's womb. I praise you, for I am fearfully and wonderfully made."

Psalm 139

For a safer world

In memory of the victims of the Grenfell Tower fire,
14 June 2017

Loving Father,
Today we remember all the victims
Of the Grenfell Tower inferno,
The many who died that night,
Those who escaped with their lives and were made homeless
And whose care was much less attentive
Than it should have been.
We pray for those who still suffer
Due to the memory of that terrible dawn
When a giant plume of smoke leaned over London
Like a reproach.

We so often feel helpless
In the face of such events
But help us, Lord, to grow in understanding
Of how such things can come about.
At times, they are simply accidents which happen
Because of pure chance, split second decisions in good faith.
But at other times, deliberate decisions
Have led to disaster: a rushed installation of equipment,
The choice of the cheapest, but least safe material,
A careless application of the health and safety rules,
An obstacle left thoughtlessly in the way.
We know too that those who have been responsible
Sometimes have told lies and hidden from the law
And only the painful determination of the victims' families
Have brought justice,
As it did for the Hillsborough 96.

Lord, we can make our world a safer, more compassionate place
By trying to understand as much as we can
About how things work, and what is safe and what is not,
By thinking about the consequences of our actions, no matter how small,
By holding to account those in power,
Being brave enough to ask the awkward questions.
It is often the poor who suffer most from accidents in the world,
Those who have no voice and no-one
To stand up for their rights,
Those who are deemed to be less important
By those who are corrupt or greedy for profit.
Lord, the cries of the poor reach heaven.
Help us to ease their suffering
By being attentive, vigilant and thoughtful
Citizens of the world.

After a terrorist attack

Loving Father,
We have heard terrible news –
People killed without warning, and again
We ask ourselves how could one human being
Do this to other human beings?
What do they hope to achieve by such violence?
How did their hearts get so dark
That they ended up doing this?

We've seen it too often –
Breaking News, early reports of casualties,
Shaky film on social media, a death toll
We wish would stop rising, sirens and armed police, panic,
People running in all directions…
Then the void gets filled with goodness –
#safespace #shelterhere, taxi drivers
Turning off the meter, blood donations, Good Samaritans
Staying with an injured one, finding a comforting word;
Flowers piling up near the police tape,
Softening the space, transforming it with words and beauty,
Candles and silence, remembrance, tearful stories
Of lives cut off with so much to offer.

Some people pray, some people feel that prayers
Are old fashioned, what's the point?
Do something practical to help, if you can.
But in this place, Lord, we cling to our prayers,
They help us to think less of ourselves and more of others,
We hope that they will help the people
Caught up in the violence. We pray for the repose
Of those who have died, may they rest in peace.
We pray for the injured and the traumatised,
We pray for those who saw things that no-one should see,
We pray for the police, the paramedics, the nurses, the doctors,
Who rush into danger when everybody else is fleeing,
Who put themselves at risk to keep us safe,
Who bind up wounds and try to heal broken bodies and spirits.

We pray for all those in the weeks, months, and years to come
Who will be haunted by what they have gone through.
We pray for those who will try to restore in them some faith
In humanity, in goodness, in everyday life.

And dare we pray for the attackers?
The person, the people, who did this? Do they get our prayers?
Today it seems very raw and we're not sure –
But Jesus, your Son, the human face of God,
Said something astonishing – "love your enemies," he said.
We've struggled from the beginning to do it,
But if God is love then that love is for everybody.
Help us today, when the sky is dark,
Not to give in to anger, or feel hate for those
Who did this terrible thing, but to keep believing
That love, not hate, is the only way.

We make this prayer through Christ our Lord.
Amen.

After a natural disaster

Loving Father,
We have heard terrible news –
People killed by the force of nature, and again
We're asking you – *why*? Why did innocent people,
Mums and dads, grans and grandads, little ones,
Have to die in the rubble, or under the wave?

We've seen all this before –
Breaking News, early reports of casualties,
Shaky film on social media, a death toll
We wish would stop rising – the water
That torrents down a bewildered street, a car
Picked up like a toy, the wind
That bends and breaks the trees, the fire
That long jumps from the forest into the suburbs, the earth
That trembles and shakes until buildings crack
And stone and timber and steel rain down onto people under their duvets,
Or watching television or cooking a meal.

Why is creation like this, Lord?
Did you really mean it *originally* to be different, a paradise,
But Adam and Eve messed up and we've been paying for it ever since?
Or is that just our best attempt to explain
Why nature is not quite right, there's a snag, a flaw in the pattern?

Some people pray when these things happen.
Some people say that prayers are old fashioned, an insult even.
What's the point? Do something useful to help,
Get your hands dirty, pull away some stones, if you can.
But in this place, Lord, we cling to our prayers.
They help us to say what's in our heart,
Inspire us to do what we can to help, even if we're far away,
Because that is what your Son, Jesus, told us to do –
Don't walk past the one who suffers – stop
And help as well as you can.

And in the meantime, we don't know
Why things are like this. A man in the Bible called Job
Had a really hard time trying to understand why bad things happened to him.
In the end he was none the wiser, and neither are we,
But he heard your voice, Lord, and that was enough for him.
He understood that he was small and would never understand the great
mysteries of nature.
Maybe that should be enough for us this morning.

Saint Peter and Saint Paul, apostles

Holy day of obligation, 29 June

Saint Peter,
Hard-working fisherman, practical man,
Called out of that life to follow Jesus,
Attracted by a new life he did not fully understand,
Chosen by Jesus to be "the rock", the reliable one,
But sometimes "rocky", getting it wrong, denying him
To a young girl when the pressure was on,
Hiding during the bedlam
Of the crucifixion, only to be found
By the risen Lord and forgiven, given three chances
To say, "I love you!" to make up for three denials
And then driven by the joy of the resurrection,
The power of the Spirit, travelling to the heart of empire,
The mighty Rome, to witness to the end;

Saint Paul,
Student of the law of Israel, guardian
Of the tradition against the newcomers, the Way,
Rounding them up, throwing them into prison, holding the coats
Of the men who stoned St Stephen, the first martyr to die like Jesus,
Until the white blinding light
On the road to Damascus and three days of complete download
Of the mind of Christ, no need to check in with anybody else,
You were now an apostle, humbled by forgiveness,
You'd seen the Risen Christ in those you persecuted,
And now, in spite of shipwreck and floggings, poverty and starvation,
Would take that message far and wide,
And, like Peter, to death in Rome;

Pray for us,
For all those who lack conviction,
For all those who make mistakes and need a way back,
For all those who need the grace to take a different path;
For the leaders of our community,
For the leaders of the Church.
We ask this through Christ our Lord.
Amen.

Before exams

Dear Lord,
Be with us as we begin our exams,
May all the work we have done bear fruit.
Help us to be calm,
To read the questions carefully
And keep an eye on the time.
Grant us a clear mind,
Protect us from all anxiety.
May we be considerate of others in the exam hall
And follow the instructions
Of those who are there to support us.
Help us to remember
That our exams are milestones
On a longer journey, as we learn
And grow into the kind of people you want us to be
Who will make a difference in the world for the better
With our knowledge, our skills
And our generous hearts.

Before sport

Lord of life,
In sport we give glory to you
With our movement and skill,
Our concentration and tactics,
Our grit and resilience,
Our consideration and fair play
Our enjoyment and celebration
Our respect for the opposition.

Lord, we are not all elite athletes,
There is not enough room for everybody
In the first fifteen, the starting line-up,
Help us to remember that we are all gifted
In different ways and never to look down
On anyone because they do not have our sporting skill,
Help us to remember that to win at all costs
Is not what we find in the Gospel,
So may we do our very best,
Play hard and fair, respect our opponents,
Respect the rules and the referee
And in all things give glory and praise to you
For the health
We enjoy.

> *"Let us open our eyes to the divine light and listen carefully to what the divine voice tells us to do when it cries out each day, 'if you hear his voice today, do not harden your hearts' (Psalms 95:7-8)."*
>
> The Rule of St Benedict, Prologue

For Europe

Feast of St Benedict,
patron of Europe,
11 July

Lord, on this the feast day
Of St Benedict, we pray for all Benedictine communities
Who follow his rule, fifteen hundred years
After he formed his first monasteries
Inspired by the Gospel to seek the balance
Between fruitful prayer and work – *ora et labora*.
The monasteries all over Europe
Were houses of prayer and praise to God
But also houses of learning, devoted to holy reading of scripture,
To preserving and copying sacred and secular texts,
To working the land, developing agriculture.

At a time of darkness
The monasteries were often the only light.
Today, the continent of Europe is still a beacon
For many people from countries
Torn apart by civil war or plagued by poverty,
People who risk everything to cross the sea in cramped and leaking dinghies,
Or cross the land huddled in stifling lorries.
Lord, inspire us to offer the welcome St Benedict
Insisted on for strangers, since in the stranger
We welcome Christ.

We pray for Europe,
Uncertain of its future,
No longer so sure of its values,
We pray for leaders who build walls
To protect their people,
Help them to see that in building walls
We become smaller, more insecure.
Inspire us again with your vision for humanity
Of unity and fellowship.

For seafarers

Sea Sunday, second Sunday in July

Lord, your friends and first followers were fishermen
Who put out onto the Sea of Galilee to make a living.
They knew the joy of a great catch, the fear of the storm
When their boat was in danger of being overwhelmed,
The long hours straining against fatigue,
The work to be done, cleaning the boat, mending the nets.
We pray today for all who work at sea, all seafarers
On the oceans of the world, transporting goods, fishing, keeping us safe.
They are often away from home for many months,
Not always working in safe conditions, not always well paid,
Not always able to pray and worship as they do at home.
Protect and comfort them
As you did with your disciples on the lake
When you calmed the storm;
Calm the troubled seas of anxiety within them,
The longing to be home with loved ones, to see children.
Mary, Mother of God, Star of the Sea,
Guide them home.

Did you know?

The Apostleship of the Sea provides practical and pastoral care to all seafarers, regardless of nationality, belief or race. Their port chaplains and volunteer ship visitors welcome seafarers, offer welfare services and advice, practical help, care and friendship. The Apostleship of the Sea in Great Britain is part of an international network known to the maritime world as Stella Maris, working in 311 ports with 216 port chaplains around the world.

Ninety per cent of world trade is transported by ship. However, the life of a modern seafarer can be dangerous and lonely. They may spend up to a year at a time away from home, separated from their families and loved ones and often working in harsh conditions. The Apostleship of the Sea relies wholly on voluntary contributions. For more information, visit http://www.apostleshipofthesea.org.uk/about-us

A blessing for leavers

Lord of friendship,
Who accompanied the disciples
On the road to Emmaus,
We gather here today to say farewell
To our pupils who are about to begin
The next stage on their journey.

Walk with them
As you walked with the uncertain disciples on the road,
Give them the comfort of your presence,
Help them to grow in understanding of your ways
and to know that you are with them
even when they do not recognise you.

Remind them
From time to time
Of the values they have learned
In this school, the memories of their years here,
The friendships formed, the lessons learned, the laughter,
The tears, the struggles, the triumphs,
The knowledge gained.

Bless them
As they seek to discover
The kind of person you want them to be,
The path in life you wish them to take,
The plans you have for them, for their welfare and not for harm,
The contribution they can make to the world
To make it more just, more kind, more compassionate
Just for them being in it.

Bless them as they leave us
With the confidence and energy of youth
To face a world which needs their integrity, their joy, their hope.
And in the words of the ancient blessing
May the road rise to meet them,
May the sun shine warm upon their faces,
And, until we meet again,
May you hold them in the palm of your hand.

"I know the plans I have for you, says the Lord,
Plans for your welfare and not for harm,
To give you a future with hope.
Then when you call upon me and come and pray to me,
I will hear you.
When you search for me, you will find me;
If you seek me with all your heart,
I will let you find me,
says the Lord."

Jeremiah 29:11-14

"As they came near the village to which they were going,
he walked ahead of them as if he were going on. But they
urged him strongly, saying, 'Stay with us, because it is
almost evening and the day is now nearly over.' So he
went in to stay with them. When he was at table with them,
he took bread, blessed and broke it, and gave it to them.
Then their eyes were opened, and they recognised him;
and he vanished from their sight. They said to each other,
'Were not our hearts burning within us while he was
talking to us on the road?'"

Luke 24:28-32

A prayer for the end of term

Loving Father,
We come to the end of another term
And give you thanks for all the chances we have had
To grow this term, for the friendships formed,
For what we have learned about ourselves
And the wonderful world we live in.

Bless our school
And those who teach and support us,
Bless those who are leaving this term,
May they find happiness in the next stage of their journey,
Bless those we will spend time with over the holiday,
Our friends and family,
Help us to appreciate what they mean to us.

Keep us safe
Over the holiday –
Near water, on the road, online.
Help us to follow our conscience and avoid situations
We know in our hearts are not right.

Inspire us
To use the opportunities we will have to grow,
To visit the wells that will nourish us
To encounter you in the beauty of nature
The depth of friendship.

We make this
And all our prayers
Through Christ our Lord,
Our friend and saviour.
Amen.

Assumption of the Blessed Virgin Mary

Holy day of obligation, 15 August

Long before 1950, when Pope Pius XII
Announced the dogma
Of the Assumption of the Blessed Virgin Mary into heaven
The faithful knew in their hearts
The truth of this mystery:
That Mary, the Mother of God,
At the moment of her earthly death was transfigured
And entered into the glory of heaven, where God is,
To pray for us as a loving mother.

*

Hail Mary
Full of grace,
The Lord is with thee.
Blessed art thou amongst women
And blessed is the fruit
Of thy womb, Jesus.

Holy Mary,
Mother of God,
Pray for us sinners: now
And at the hour of our death.
Amen.

III

PRAYER LIFE IN SCHOOLS:
IDEAS, RESOURCES AND
CASE STUDIES

Some key terms

Collective worship

Collective Worship is a legal term and not a phrase which occurs often in Church documents. In the UK, it is still the law that children in maintained schools should take part in a daily act of collective worship or religious observance. In England the law is widely ignored and Ofsted has stopped monitoring compliance. However, for Catholic and Church of England schools, a daily act of worship is more about Christian identity than compliance with any secular law. As we noted in Part I, prayer is the "daily bread" for the Christian community, a matter of routine. Dioceses will have their own guidance on collective worship which should be followed. Guidance from the Diocese of Leeds offers the following definition: "Collective Worship is concerned with giving glory, honour, praise and thanks to God. It is our loving response, in word and action, to God's invitation to enter into relationship made possible through the work of Jesus Christ and the witness of the Holy Spirit."[1] Schools should be careful to distinguish between assemblies and collective worship. Assemblies are often opportunities for passing on information to pupils or for the presentation of worthy but secular themes. Assemblies can include an act of worship but the difference between the two should always be clear, especially if you have a diocesan inspector sitting at the back of the hall.

In most schools, the daily act of worship will take place in a classroom or form room. Again, your diocese may well have guidelines on the format. The prayers in Part II of this book will hopefully provide one element of a daily collective worship. Other elements could be a reading from scripture, a reflection, prayers of intercession, or one of the activities suggested below, begun and ended with the sign of the cross.

Devotional prayer

There are two main types of prayer which might be helpful for those who lead and support the prayer life of the school. The Canadian Catholic priest and best-selling author Ronald Rolheiser sums up the difference as follows: "Theologians make an important distinction between what they call 'devotional' and 'liturgical' prayer. Devotional prayer, they tell us, is private in nature and is meant to help sustain us personally on the spiritual journey. Liturgical prayer, by contrast, is public by nature, the Church's prayer (not our own), is universal in scope, and is intended for the needs of the world."[2] Devotional prayer is also known as "affective prayer" – prayer that's about us and our needs, with the intention of bringing ourselves and our needs to God. Liturgical prayer is also known as "priestly prayer" which is not about us, it is about the world and for the world.

Rolheiser provides some examples which help us to understand the difference. You could have a thousand people sitting in meditation together or saying the rosary and that is still devotional or affective prayer. On the other hand, one person might be praying the Divine Office alone at home, or a priest might be celebrating Mass at a kitchen table, and that is still public, liturgical prayer. Devotional prayer has many forms – and when one isn't working we can move on to another form – but it has one aim, according to Rolheiser, which is "to draw us and our loved ones into deeper intimacy with Christ."[3] The key to prayer, as Rolheiser learned once from a retreat master, "is to turn from ourselves to God."[4]

Liturgy

Liturgy is a term which you may often hear in school so it is important to have a good working understanding of what it means. *The New Dictionary of Theology* offers the following definition: "Within the Roman Catholic tradition, liturgy designates the official public worship of the Church. To call it official is to say that it is authorized by and takes place in communion with the local bishop according to the norms approved by the Roman See."[5] Liturgy is the "official" prayer life and worship of the Church, not prayers we make up ourselves, not the prayers in this book, but the prayers and rituals which have been handed on and approved by the Church. There are many different types of liturgy, such as the baptismal liturgy, Liturgy of the Hours, liturgy of penance, liturgy of the Eucharist.
The most common liturgy used in schools will probably be the liturgy of the Eucharist, the Mass. Liturgy should not be confused with assemblies or collective worship in school, which are often put together by staff from different sources.

Liturgical prayer

Liturgical prayer is found in all liturgies but one type of liturgical prayer which is increasingly being used in some schools is the Liturgy of the Hours, or Divine Office. This is the official prayer of the Church and forms the basis of the prayer life of monastic communities. Rolheiser draws our attention to Lauds (morning prayer) and Vespers (evening prayer) as the ordinary priestly prayer of the laity. "Unlike private prayer and contemplation, in which we should change methods whenever praying becomes dry or sterile, Lauds and Vespers are prayers of the universal Church that are in essence intended to be communal and priestly. We pray them… to invoke God's blessing upon the world."[6] See below for more details.

Liturgical year

"Christ's saving work is celebrated in sacred memory by the Church on fixed days throughout the course of the year. Each week on the day called the Lord's Day the Church commemorates the Lord's resurrection. Once a year at Easter the Church honours the resurrection of the Lord and his blessed passion with the utmost solemnity. In fact through the yearly cycle the Church unfolds the entire mystery of Christ and keeps the anniversaries of the saints."[7] The General Norms for the Liturgical Year and Calendar (GNLY) is the Church document which introduces the Church's celebration of the liturgical year and how it is celebrated.

The liturgical year begins on the First Sunday of Advent and runs through to the solemnity of Christ the King. The liturgical seasons are Advent, Christmas, Ordinary Time, Lent, Easter Triduum, Easter Season and again Ordinary Time. The seasons are associated with four main liturgical colours: white is used in the seasons of Easter and Christmas and on certain feast days; red is used on Palm Sunday of the Lord's Passion and Good Friday, on Pentecost Sunday, on certain feast days and on celebrations of the martyrs; green is used in Ordinary Time; violet (or purple) is used in the seasons of Advent and Lent. Schools are now commonly displaying the colours of the liturgical year in classroom prayer stations or in reception and assembly halls. For more information on the liturgical year, please visit http://www.liturgyoffice.org.uk/Calendar/Info/background1.shtml.

Sacred scripture

There are many different translations and versions of sacred scripture and not all are suitable for use in school. The Bishops' Conference of England and Wales has approved the following versions of scripture for use in liturgy: Revised Standard Version, Jerusalem Bible, New Jerusalem Bible, New Revised Standard Version and Good News (which may be used for Masses with children). Catholic schools will be advised by their diocese to use one of these translations in school. The Church of England does not authorise translations as such but offers advice on which translations might be suitable for use in liturgy – for more information, visit https://www.churchofengland.org/prayer-worship/worship/texts/the-calendar/lect/scriptver.aspx.

Creative ideas for prayer life in school

Active contemplation

Active contemplation, or Ignatian contemplation, was taught by Saint Ignatius of Loyola, the founder of the Society of Jesus (The Jesuits). Ignatius valued the role of imagination in prayer, trusting that it was one way in which God communicated with human beings. The form of prayer he developed seems simple enough. You take a scene from scripture and imagine yourself in it as a participant. With pupils, it would be better if someone led them into the contemplation after the passage was read aloud, inviting them to place themselves among the sights and sounds, smells and tastes, the people, of the scene. As well as reflecting on the story, pupils could be invited to ask themselves which character they most associate with and why. Ignatius encouraged people to return to the same passage of scripture more than once. When the pupils have explored where they see themselves in the story ask them to quietly pray about the questions which arise in their hearts. In Advent and Lent you could then conclude with the prayers in Part II, which are based on the scripture readings for that that time of year. Another form of this approach is Godly Play (see: case studies below).

Art

Art can be a very powerful aid to prayer, especially when used in conjunction with scripture. There are several good websites which make great art available online such as https://www.wikiart.org/. If you are reading the parable of the sower, for example (Matthew 13:1-23) you could have up on the whiteboard, if you have one, the image of The Sower by Vincent van Gogh – https://www.wikiart.org/en/Search/van%20gogh%20sower. Having read the passage from scripture you could ask the pupils to explore the painting with you and discuss which aspects of the scripture passage the painter is trying to bring out. In Van Gogh's painting the sun is the radiant focus, suggesting the fruitful power of God the Father, the source of life.

Beatitudes

The Beatitudes challenge each generation of Christians to reflect on what persons and actions they consider to be important or blessed. Pope Francis, in his homily at a Mass in Sweden in 2016, proposed six new beatitudes for the current age. He said,

> The Beatitudes are in some sense the Christian's identity card. They identify us as followers of Jesus. We are called to be blessed, to be followers of Jesus, to confront the troubles and anxieties of our age with the spirit and love of Jesus.

Thus we ought to be able to recognize and respond to new situations with fresh spiritual energy. Blessed are those who remain faithful while enduring evils inflicted on them by others, and forgive them from their heart. Blessed are those who look into the eyes of the abandoned and marginalized, and show them their closeness. Blessed are those who see God in every person, and strive to make others also discover him. Blessed are those who protect and care for our common home. Blessed are those who renounce their own comfort in order to help others. Blessed are those who pray and work for full communion between Christians. All these are messengers of God's mercy and tenderness, and surely they will receive from him their merited reward.[8]

Pope Francis, Homily November 2016

The class or form group could write their own set of beatitudes: which persons or actions in today's society do they consider to be blessed by God?

Book of Intentions

Pupils have an instinct to pray for their intentions and for other people (see: types of prayer in Part I). Depending on the culture and practice of the school, pupils may not be comfortable praying aloud for their intentions. A good way to allow them to pray in this way is to invite them to write their intentions in a special Book of Intentions which stays in the classroom or form room. The book should have a notable cover to help it stand out from other books.

Candle

A good focal point for prayer is a single candle. You will of course need to be attentive to the health and safety practice in your schools. Some schools won't permit candles, some will. An alternative could be an LED "candle" which is just as effective. If you're able to gather your class or form group around you then a candle in the middle of the gathering can be a helpful focal point for prayer, especially silent prayer or meditation. A candle can also be passed around a group and the person who holds the candle can pray for their intentions or the group can pray for them. The candle reminds us that Jesus Christ is the light of the world.

Centering prayer

There has been a great deal of interest in recent years in the practice of mindfulness. Many schools have now introduced mindfulness into the curriculum, with widely reported positive benefits for the pupils. For Catholic and Church of England schools, I would urge caution. Mindfulness has its roots in the Buddhist tradition and was adapted in the 1970s in America by Jon Kabat-Zinn, who developed a meditation-based programme to help support people suffering from chronic pain. It was adapted further by cognitive behaviour therapists to help people with depression. It has been adapted further for widespread general use, including use in schools. Mindfulness has been defined as being more fully aware of your own experience in the present moment.

I only urge caution because, while mindfulness is an efficacious way to reduce stress and perception of pain, it is not Christian and in the meantime there is a very long tradition of Christian meditative practice, arguably going all the way back to Jesus, as we discovered in Part I. In America in the 1970s a group of Trappist monks developed Centering prayer which was designed to introduce ordinary people to the Christian contemplative tradition.

Centering prayer is a receptive method of silent prayer that prepares us to experience God's presence within us, closer than breathing, closer than thinking, closer than consciousness itself. This method of prayer is both a relationship with God and a discipline to foster that relationship. The method is deceptively simple and very suitable for use with pupils in school. Essentially, centering prayer involves being silent and still, beginning with an act of faith or prayer to the Holy Spirit. In silence, which has been described as God's first language, we can begin to set aside our own agendas, our ego, and pay attention to the presence of God. Distractions and thoughts will arise, but we shouldn't worry about that, it's a sign that we are alive and mentally active. When thoughts come the advice is to gently say an interior "sacred word" of our choice – it could be Jesus, My Lord, Peace, Love, Holy Spirit. Keep it simple and only use it to bring the intention back to resting in God's presence. It is not a mantra to be said throughout. It would be advisable to receive some training on centering prayer and better if it was adopted as a whole school practice. For more information, please visit https://www.contemplativeoutreach.org/category/category/centering-prayer

Another useful site for general information about Christian meditation is The World Community for Christian Meditation at http://wccm.org/content/meditation-children-new

Collect

The collect is a prayer very familiar to Catholics but it is very easy to overlook. In every Mass there is a collect, a very short prayer, just before the Liturgy of the Word. These prayers have a set format and structure. Padraig O'Tuama, the leader of the Corrymeela community in Northern Ireland, has drawn attention to this humble prayer form and has written a selection of his own collects. He describes the format as follows:

> The collect has beautiful form, like a haiku of intention. It has five folds. The person speaks to God; the person names part of the story of God; the person names their desire – only one desire; and then the person praying gives a reason why this is the one desire they name. This fourth fold echoes the first two; the name and the named story of God. And then the person finishes their prayer – with an Amen, or with a small bird of praise. [9]

Padraig's beautiful collects can be found in *Daily Prayer with the Corrymeela Community* (Canterbury Press, 2017). For an example of a collect in this book, see "For freedom from anxiety" in Part II. Why not try inviting the pupils to write their own collect, or even a sequence of collects on a theme?

Daily news

Prayer should be real, grounded in the everyday experiences of the pupils and our world. There are a number of good websites which cover current affairs for schools, such as http://theday.co.uk/. News stories can be used for reflection on matters of right and wrong, social justice, celebrations of courage and so on. Prayers of intercession will then naturally arise from the stories.

Divine Office

The Divine Office, which is also known as the Breviary or the Liturgy of the Hours (Liturgia Horarum), or Work of God (Opus Dei), is the official public prayer of the Church. This liturgical prayer forms the basis of the prayer life within Christian monasteries. Lay people are under no obligation to say the breviary, but some do, especially Lauds (morning prayer) and Vespers (evening prayer). As noted above, the main difference between liturgical and devotional prayer is that in liturgical prayer we are less concerned for our own needs and moods. We join the universal Church in its prayer for the world. As Ronald Rolheiser explains, "Whenever we pray Lauds or Vespers, we take on a universal voice. We are no longer just a private individual praying: we are the voice, body and soul of the earth itself, continuing the high priesthood of Christ, offering prayers and entreaties, aloud and in silent tears, to God for the sake of the world." [10] There has been a good deal of interest in the prayer of the Church in schools in recent years, especially in schools with a religious order foundation. Lauds in particular would be suitable for use in schools at the beginning of the day. The Psalms could be said antiphonally, as they are in monasteries, with one half of the class or assembly, saying one verse, then the other. It will of course depend on the age of the pupils and the culture of the school, but this is well worth exploring as an option for prayer. The daily prayers can be found at www. universalis.com

Do without day

The three 'Lenten Practices' are prayer, fasting and almsgiving. They are in fact central to Christian life and not just during Lent. Jesus gives advice on all three during the Sermon on the Mount in Matthew's Gospel. Fasting was traditionally seen as a physical deprivation during Lent, like going hungry, or giving up sugar in your tea. Going hungry so as to appreciate how much food we have and to pray for those who have much less is a good thing, but in a school setting needs to be handled sensitively, especially with the rise of eating disorders among young people. A more general understanding of "fasting" could be to do without a non-essential for one day in the week, such as the mobile phone, social media or the Playstation. The pupils could share what they have done without and use that as a prayer to appreciate what is important in life.

Examen of consciousness

Examen is a technique of prayerful reflection on the day, or recent events, in order to try and discern God's presence in our lives. The method presented in this prayer is adapted from a technique described by St Ignatius of Loyola in his great work, the *Spiritual Exercises*. St Ignatius founded the Jesuit order, which today is the largest male religious order in the Catholic Church, with some 16,000 priests, brothers and novices worldwide. For more information on the Jesuits, visit http://jesuits. org/aboutus. For more information on Jesuit/Ignatian spirituality, including more advice on the Daily Examen, visit http://www.ignatianspirituality.com/. This prayer can easily be adapted as an Examen for the end of the week or end of the day.

Extemporaneous prayer

Extemporaneous prayer is prayer which is spontaneous and unscripted. You may have heard this type of prayer at the beginning of a meeting, or a meal, when someone is asked to say a prayer. The prayer is usually for blessing or petition. Pupils and staff may need some time and encouragement to become comfortable with this sort of prayer. It will depend on the culture of the school, but when it becomes established it is often a very popular way to turn to God in the everyday events of life. It reminds us that to pray to God is natural and we can and should use our own words.

Five finger prayer

This very simple prayer of petition has been popularised by Pope Francis. Use the left hand for prayer intentions as follows –

Thumb – for those closest to us, our friends and family

Index finger, the pointer – for those who instruct, our teachers, grant them wisdom

Middle finger, the tallest – for our leaders, school governors

Ring finger, the weakest – for the sick and those with problems

Pinky, smallest finger – when we have prayed for everyone else, we pray for ourselves and our needs.

Gift of God

I once took part in an exercise called "positive strokes" when everybody in the room had a blank piece of paper taped to their back. The idea was to go round and write one positive thing about each person on the paper. At the end you had a collection of comments which were affirming and sometimes surprising. With careful preparation, a version of this could work in school. You distribute a card or piece of paper with each pupil's name written on it, with the phrase, Gift of God. Everybody is invited to write one positive word or phrase describing the person, focusing on their strengths and gifts. This should be done in silence, or with some reflective music playing, to emphasise the prayerful nature of the activity. Pupils aren't allowed to see their own card. This is a way of looking for the good and positive in everybody and letting them know that they are gifted. Collect in all the cards. You may want to just check to make sure there are no silly comments and then they can be given out in the course of a simple prayer service.

Guided reflection or meditation

Guided meditation is a prayer technique in which the participants are led through various experiences. Unlike active contemplation (above) where the imagination of the one praying is led into a passage of scripture by the Holy Spirit, guided meditation involves deliberately taking the participants through the stages of an inner journey to a different place or point of reflection. In Part II, "A liturgy of stones" is a guided meditation. In school, it tends to work best when one person reads the meditation aloud (doesn't have to be the teacher, but some experience and sensitivity is required) and the pupils allow themselves to be led into the meditation. Caution again is advised when looking for examples of guided reflection. There is a lot of material available for practices like yoga which will be non-Christian. A good place to start your search would be www.catechistsjourney.loyolapress.com.

Hymn practice

Singing is a wonderful way to pray: it is communal, physical and fun. When I was a headteacher in a Catholic school, I became concerned at one point that the pupils were not singing at Mass. This was a secondary school, so perhaps it was no longer "cool" for the teenagers to sing with enthusiasm the way they did when they were younger. The solution we came up with was to get Year 7 (11-2-year-olds) together for hymn practice or a singing assembly. Without the older pupils, they sang their hearts out. This can then be gradually extended to the older year groups so singing gradually becomes a normal part of the prayer life of the school. In the Abbey Primary School in Birmingham they called it Songs of Praise. I had the good fortune to be walking round the school with the headteacher as this was just starting, so we stayed for a while. The pupils nearly took the roof off! I couldn't quite believe the volume and enthusiasm they generated. So have a word with the musicians in the school and get the pupils singing.

Intercessions

As outlined in Part I, intercession is one of the five main types of prayer. Pupils could be invited to write their own intercessions, or prayers for the needs of the world, our country, the local community, their friends and family. Prayers of intercession used at Mass are sometimes called bidding prayers.

Lectio Divina

Another way to use scripture is to follow the traditional method developed in monastic communities, known as Lectio Divina. The case studies below include two examples of the use of Lectio in schools which explain some of the basic principles and the impact on pupils. For more information on Lectio Divina in practice, see the case studies below or visit Contemplative Outreach at https://www.contemplativeoutreach.org/category/category/lectio-divina. The link between Lectio Divina and meditation is very important. The final stage of Lectio Divina is contemplation, otherwise known as resting in God, or listening to the word of God in our lives. Lectio Divina is the most traditional way of cultivating contemplative prayer.

Letter to God

A good way to pray, or to communicate with God is to write him a letter, like Lulu did. This not only keeps alive an ancient practice of communication which has all but died out in the age of instant messaging, but it gives pupils a little longer to think about what they want to say to God. This could work as a project over a week, perhaps during Advent or Lent. With permission from the pupils, letters could be shared or displayed. The letters should be open and honest, encouraging questions.

Litany

A litany is another very ancient devotional practice in the Catholic tradition. A litany is a series of petitions used in Church services or processions, usually recited by the clergy and responded to in a recurring formula by the people. The response is often "Pray for us", as in the "Litany to Mary, Mother of God" in Part II. You might consider writing a class litany. You could start with a theme or focus, like the God of creation, and ask the pupils to think of different phrases to explore this theme, for example: God of the mighty seas, Lord of the changing skies, God of quiet growth. You can then create a response, which could simply be "Pray for us", but many modern litanies have expanded responses, such as "Thank you for the wonders of our world."

Objects

A simple everyday object can lead to very fruitful meditation (see: Meditation on a one pound coin in Part II). Once you've chosen your object you could ask the pupils to tell the story of the object, or ask it questions, or ask God what part this object plays in his plan of creation. Think of the imaginative possibilities of a leaf, an acorn, a glove, a pebble, a shoe, a key. You could extend this idea by asking the pupils to bring in an object which means something special to them.

One word prayer

Ask everyone in the class/form group to think of one word which comes to mind after listening to a passage of scripture, or reflecting on the theme of the day. Go round the class and ask each pupil to say their one word, finish with the sign of the cross. When I visited St Thomas More in Crewe to interview some pupils, I finished by asking them to think of one word which came to mind when they thought of God or prayer. We went around the group and each pupil said their word – love, courage, amazing, majestic, hope, presence, comfort, miraculous, wonderful. The result was a simple, beautiful prayer, with every pupil involved.

Prayer bag

Some schools, like St Louis in Somerset (see: below) have developed the practice of the "prayer bag". This is literally a bag in which the children take home some artefacts from the prayer station so that their parents also have an opportunity to pray or to understand more about what is involved in prayer. In some cases, the pupils take home a book of intentions and write their own prayer in it before returning it to school (see: Zofia's prayer, below).

Prayer basket

A variation on the prayer bag is the prayer basket. In one school, each pupil was asked to write a prayer for the beginning of the school day. All the prayers were kept in the prayer basket and the teacher used a different prayer each day. This could be done at different times of the liturgical year, such as Advent and Lent.

Prayer journal

The prayer journal is something which is being used in some schools. Sometimes it's called a learning journal. A journal of this kind is a place where pupils can write down their thoughts and reflections for the week (see: "Friday morning" prayer in Part II). It could be a place to write down favourite words or song lyrics or lines from prayers. This could also be a good place for pupils new to the school to reflect on their own faith tradition or background, especially if they have little experience of a faith environment. This may not work in every school with every pupil but some version of this is worth considering to encourage reflection among the pupils.

Prayer station

A feature of many schools now is a prayer station or prayer focus in each classroom/ form room. The essential ingredients of the prayer station may be prescribed by your diocese, so please check with them first. Typically, a prayer station will have a cloth of some kind in the liturgical colour of the season. There is often a crucifix, a Bible, a candle (health and safety permitting, perhaps an LED 'candle'), a small statue of Our Lady or one of the saints, holy water, a book of intentions, or prayer board, rosary beads (see: below) and other holy artefacts. This station provides a helpful focus for morning prayer and a constant reminder throughout the day of the importance of prayer. More innovative ideas can be found at http://www.prayerspacesinschools.com/

Register prayer

In some schools, the class register is used to focus the prayer intentions of the class/ form on a different pupil each day. Beginning at the top, the teacher puts a pupil's name on the board each day during the taking of the register. The pupil is asked if they have any prayer intentions, but if not, or if they don't want to say them out loud, the class simply prays for them and all their needs.

Schools of prayer

There are many different schools of prayer, mostly associated with the religious orders of the Catholic Church, such as the Jesuits, Benedictines and Franciscans. Some study of these different schools, or approaches, to prayer would be useful, depending on the age and background of the pupils. The prayer life in schools which have a religious order foundation will tend to be inspired and informed by that order, so for example in Jesuit schools the practice of Examen will be quite common and in Benedictine schools you may see Lectio Divina. All schools of course are free to choose from the rich variety of prayer resources available from the tradition. In practice, most schools probably have a "pick and mix" approach, taking what is most useful for them from the different schools.

Sin bin

During Advent and Lent, many schools will hold services of reconciliation. In preparation for these services in my last school, we invited the pupils to examine their conscience and consider the times when their relations with others were harmful. They wrote down what they were sorry for, or who they wished to be reconciled with, and these pieces of paper were gathered in and brought to the service. During the service, all the pieces of paper were taken outside and burned in a brazier. This of course has to be very carefully supervised and the correct risk assessments need to be undertaken but the symbolism can be so powerful. God does not hold grudges and neither should we. God's forgiveness is available to a sorry heart and the weight, or guilt, of sin can be released. Just make sure there's a fire extinguisher nearby!

Sixty second prayer

In one Catholic school I heard about on my travels, I was told that during Lent the Muslim pupils said that there was not much evidence of regular prayer, compared to their own practice. They challenged the school to pray more and the result was the sixty second prayer. For the rest of Lent, three times during the school day a bell rang and the entire school observed sixty seconds of silent prayer. To begin with, the end of the day was quite challenging since the parents used to gather outside and have a chat. The caretaker went out to warn them about the sixty second silence, so everybody took part. This simple but effective silent prayer has proved so popular that the school is looking to introduce it all year round.

The Jesus prayer

This prayer is one of the oldest and shortest prayers in the Christian tradition. It is based on the words of the tax collector (see: Part I), "Lord Jesus Christ, Son of God, be merciful to me a sinner." The prayer was initially used by monks who wanted to follow St Paul's instruction to pray continuously. In modern life, it is used as a short prayer through the day to bring to mind God's presence in our lives. It is a useful "weapon" against unwelcome thoughts, since when you are saying the prayer, other thoughts are silenced.

The rosary

The rosary is one of the most popular prayer devotions in the Catholic tradition. The intention of praying the rosary is to bring to mind the main events in salvation history. A beginner's guide to the rosary can be found at https://www.catholicity.com/prayer/rosary.html. In simple theological terms, it is worth explaining to the pupils that in the Catholic tradition Mary the Mother of God has a very esteemed place of veneration, but she is not worshipped like God. We ask her to pray for our needs. In our devotional or affective prayers, it sometimes helps to use a given format or formula. When I spoke to pupils in schools some of them liked to have prayers to turn to in times of crisis. In the rosary, the repetition of the Hail Mary acts as an aid to meditation on the mystery we are contemplating. It is very close in some respects to Lectio Divina, with a focus on scenes from scripture, or the Catholic tradition. The rosary is another traditional devotion which is enjoying something of a revival in schools, which illustrates the grace and wisdom associated with the practice. For more creative ideas on how to pray the rosary, visit http://catechistsjourney.loyolapress.com/2016/10/creative-ways-to-pray-the-rosary/.

Traditional prayers

There are many wonderful prayers in the Catholic Christian tradition which have been the mainstay of generations of Christian lay people. Some of these prayers will be more accessible to young people than others, depending on their age and religious background. However, as part of the overall experience of a praying Catholic or Anglican community I would recommend incorporating these prayers into the prayer routine of the school. A good selection can be found at www.liturgyoffice.org.uk > Prayer.

What kind of person do you really want to be?

A variation on the Letter to God project is to answer on a postcard the question Pope Benedict XVI asked the young people when he visited Britain in 2010, "What kind of person do you really want to be?" In my last school we invited all the pupils to answer this question literally on a postcard which we had printed for the occasion. It was done as a Lent exercise and the pupils were given several weeks to draft their answers. It is important to stress that the question is not, "What would you like to be when you're older?" It's not an exercise in careers education (although it would contribute to that). It's an exercise in reflecting on the kinds of qualities which are worth developing. When all pupils in the school had written their final answers on a postcard, they were brought up at the offertory procession in the final school Mass before the Easter break. Many were displayed around the school. Pupils had the choice of remaining anonymous or adding their names. I noticed in subsequent weeks that these displays attracted a lot of attention. We also used the answers, which were often very moving, in assemblies and prayer times for the rest of the year.

You did it to me

The story is told of St Teresa of Calcutta who was once asked about the essence of prayer. She took the hand of the person who asked her the question and pointing at one finger at a time said, "You did it to me." This was a reference to the Judgement of the Nations in Matthew's Gospel (25:31-46). This reminds us that the essence of Christian life according to the story in Matthew's Gospel is how we treat the vulnerable and dependent, since whatever we do to them, we do to God. The pupils could say this prayer after seeing it done by their teacher. When they point at their fingers they are also reminded that it is hands that are associated with doing, as in the prayer of St Teresa of Avila which says that Christ has no hands on earth now but ours.

Top tips for praying with pupils

∗ Make sure prayers are **led by pupils**. Involve as many of the class or form group as possible in the planning and delivery of prayers, preferably all of them if you can.

∗ **Ask the pupils** about prayer, what they like and don't like, what works and what doesn't work.

∗ Invite the pupils to **write their own prayers**. If this is not part of the culture of the school then to begin with it may be awkward, especially for older pupils. But as it becomes the norm it is remarkable how easily pupils take to this.

∗ Keep the prayer as **accessible** as possible, keep it simple.

∗ Don't be afraid of **silence**. It may be uncomfortable to begin with but pupils will soon appreciate, respect and value silence. Ideally, every prayer time should have a period of silence.

∗ **Keep it real**. Use the experiences of the pupils, use the news, use everyday life.

∗ **Sacred space** is helpful, but often prayer sessions/collective worship need to be held in a classroom so the idea of **sacred time** can be more helpful, while trying to develop the idea that all time and all space is in fact sacred.

∗ Prayer is above all about growing in **friendship with God**, it's not something that can be weighed and measured. Prayer is a welcome relief from targets and key performance indicators. Just be yourself, your real self, with your God who loves you. Enjoy the deep rest it brings.

Case studies from schools, colleges and universities

Advent calendar at Leeds Trinity University

Hannah Hayward is the Coordinating Lay Chaplain, Leeds Trinity University, one of the group of Catholic universities and colleges in England. She explained to me an innovative approach to Advent which has captured the imagination of the students:

We created an interactive Advent calendar for the campus. We created 25 A3 poster "windows" around the campus, each one numbered 1-25 and with a golden box attached to it. Inside each box was a handful of chocolates, and a "Did You know?" Christmas fact, a "What can you do?" practical challenge for the day, and a relevant piece of Scripture. We tried to make the fact, challenge and scripture reference linked to each other. For one box, for example, we had: "Did you know: Christmas lights were invented in 1882 by Edward Hibberd Johnson?"; "Turn off the lights when you leave a room empty today"; Scripture "I am the light of the world" says the Lord (John 8:12). Advent calendar "windows" were placed all over campus by student volunteers. Occasional windows included a Christmas quiz question, and if students tweeted their answer to the Chaplaincy they received a free edible prize. We covered the project on social media platforms Instagram, Twitter and Facebook.

As well as being a visible sign of Advent around the campus, this was a particularly good project for engaging students and staff. We gathered material for inside the boxes by going round the canteen at lunchtime and asking students and staff to suggest Christmas facts, suggested practical acts of kindness, famous scripture quotations, and so on. As well as giving us some great material, it also prompted some fantastic conversations with students, especially when discussing possible acts of kindness. We also contacted colleagues in History, Theology and Religious Studies, Media, the Library, for interesting Christmas facts and got some great responses. This helped to promote the idea around various departments, and it kept the material varied, involving the wisdom of our academic staff. Obviously, the amount of practical work involved (lots of cutting, sticking and pinning!) needed a team of volunteers too, so we ordered some pizza in after the Sunday evening Mass, and invited students to stay behind to help. Lots stayed, and we had a great evening of fellowship and creativity together.

Arrupe Programme at St Aloysius' College, Glasgow

Lyn McWilliams, the Director of Christian Formation at St Aloysius' College in Glasgow, a member of the international network of Jesuit schools, explains the origins of the college's outreach programme:

In 1973, Fr Pedro Arrupe gave his landmark speech to the Tenth International Congress of Jesuit Alumni in Valencia, Spain. Delivered in the wake of Pope Paul VI's *Populorum Progressio*, the Father General's words brought the Ignatian tradition firmly back to its roots and called upon those involved in the works of the Society to indeed go where the need was greatest. In this hard-hitting address, the man who had witnessed the worst that humans can do to one another at the time of the bombing of Hiroshima said:

> Today our prime educational objective must be to form men and women for others; men and women who will live not for themselves but for God and his Christ – for the God-man who lived and died for all the world; men and women who cannot even conceive of love of God which does not include love for the least of their neighbours; men and women completely convinced that love of God which does not issue in justice for others is a farce.

So, was born a new era in which those involved in Jesuit schools, universities and spirituality, those aware of the forgotten and the marginalised, embraced Fr Arrupe's challenge and began once again to go where the need is greatest. Throughout the global Ignatian community countless outreach programmes testify to the power of those words uttered in 1973. For the outsider this may simply appear to be an altruistic venture which seeks to address poverty, injustice and stereotypes. While this is not an unworthy goal, there is more to it still, because such endeavours also embrace the Ignatian Paradigm of Experience, Reflection and Action.

In 2006, inspired by the work being done in many Jesuit schools and universities in North America, staff at St Aloysius' College in Glasgow, led by Outreach Co-ordinator Julie McWilliams, decided to build on a long tradition of service and initiate the Arrupe Programme. The plan called for senior students in the sixth form to go out into the community one afternoon a week. The goal was to place these young people in a diverse range of environments, including care homes for the elderly, projects supporting asylum seekers, schools for children with additional support needs and programmes such as food banks and schools in areas of social deprivation. Those participating were given special training, including health and safety, child protection, skills for working with specific groups such as the elderly and guidance in Ignatian reflection, more properly known as the process of discernment.

A key element of the Arrupe Programme is the journal. In the model of Experience, Reflection, Action, participants complete a journal following each week's placement. The purpose of this is not to provide a list of activities completed, but, more importantly, to reflect on where they have found God present in their experience. This process of discernment is integral to the programme, not an added extra. And sometimes God is found in the most unexpected places, not only in successes, but in failures, not just in the things that go to plan, but in those things which go pear-shaped under the guidance of the Holy Spirit. It is truly about finding God in all things. At a recent staff retreat, sixth form student Cait Murphy spoke about her placement at a school for children with additional support needs. Her words are used with permission.

Hi, my name is Cait Murphy and today I'm going to talk to you about my Arrupe placement. However, before I get into all the details, I would like to talk to you about a young boy called Jack. Jack is blind, wheelchair-bound, almost completely deaf, tube fed and has many other complex disabilities which require 24/7 care. Some people would call Jack a burden, a liability. Some would even say that he should have been aborted. However, I want to tell you about the inspiration that Jack brings to me every Wednesday afternoon. The things that people do not see about him; his laugh, cheeky grin and sheer excitement for life. Jack is one of the many, many reasons that my experience of the Arrupe Programme has been such an amazing one.

Since August of this school year, I have been volunteering at Hazelwood School. All of the students have some sort of visual impairment and most also have hearing impairments and other severe disabilities. The school itself is incredible, from the navigational rails to cupboards for wheelchairs built into the walls so the children do not trip. Musical instruments are a part of their outdoor playground and there is a swimming pool where the children have the chance of getting out of their wheelchairs. It is certainly worthy of all the architectural awards it has won. The class that I have been placed in is for children who have extremely severe disabilities that require much more hands-on care. They are all in wheelchairs and none of them are actually able to speak, but they are some of the most hilarious and joyful children I have ever had the pleasure of meeting. Seeing them sitting laughing their heads off at the simplest things really lights up my day in a way that I never thought was possible.

Meeting them has been a real eye-opener for me in that, for them, a good day is being able to reach out and point to a certain number when asked or being able to nod their head when asked a question. When I have been having a bad day because of a poor grade on a homework assignment and then I go to Hazelwood and I see that one of the boys has had his third seizure of the day it really puts my problems into perspective. Because of my time at Hazelwood, I have become much more grateful for the privileged life that I have. In addition to their disabilities, there are those who go home to unstable home lives, some even without parents to see. Hazelwood is not just a school to them but can also be a place of refuge where they can relax and see their friends and not worry about their disability. This is only one of the qualities that make this school so unique. The staff show a deep care for each individual child, treating them as if they were their own.

When I see the effort that the staff put into caring for the children it has really helped me to see God in a way that I have never even considered before. Going and volunteering at Hazelwood has helped me to re-evaluate my relationship with God. Before I struggled with seeing how an all-loving God could render these children so helpless. However, when I see the joy on their faces during music time or when one of them manages to sit up unsupported I can really see how God is truly present in the lives of all these wonderful children. To finish with an insight from Fr Arrupe: "Nowadays the world doesn't need words, but lives which cannot be explained except through faith and love for Christ's poor.

Corpus Christi procession at Prior Park College, Bath

The feast of Corpus Christi ("The Body of Christ") is celebrated on the Sunday following Trinity Sunday. This feast celebrates the real presence of the body and blood of Jesus Christ in the Eucharist. After Mass on the feast day there is by tradition a public procession of the Blessed Sacrament, with the consecrated host carried in a monstrance by the priest. The procession ends with Benediction, a blessing of the Blessed Sacrament. During the reformation and up until the early twentieth century, such processions were suppressed since the reformers did not believe in the real presence of Christ in the Eucharist. In recent times, the practice has seen something of a revival in parishes and schools. A Corpus Christi procession has long been part of the calendar at Prior Park College in Bath. Charlotte Cummins, Senior Deputy, explains:

Coming together in procession as the People of God is long established in Catholic tradition. For those taking part, there is a sense of unity with the wider Church as people of many backgrounds walk together, and also of pilgrimage as the physical effort of the journey reflects our own journey with Christ. For those who simply observe the procession, perhaps with interest or curiosity, they see the People of God bear public witness to their faith. It is no surprise, then, that a Eucharistic Procession on the Feast of Corpus Christi is among the most popular of all the annual processions.

When the Benedictine Bishop Baines managed to purchase the Prior Park estate, positioned high on one of the hills of Bath, shortly after the Emancipation and establish a College for the education of Catholic boys, he was keen to let it shine forth in witness. Although a very different school now, we still use the image found in Matthew 5:14, "You are the light of the world. A city built on a hill-top cannot be hidden." In June 1831, just a year after taking possession of Prior Park, Bishop Baines held the first Corpus Christi procession in its grounds. By doing so, he established a tradition which continues to this day.

As a boarding school, we celebrate Mass each Sunday in our chapel of Our Lady of the Snows. On the Feast of Corpus Christi, we invite members of all the local parishes to join us. This year we were fortunate to have both our Junior and Senior Chapel choirs leading our music both during Mass and as we processed afterwards to the Mansion steps where students, staff and friends of the College knelt in Eucharistic Adoration. The canopy used in the procession is the same one used by Bishop Baines all those years ago. Following a short Benediction, we ask God's blessing on the city of Bath nestled in the valley below. In this way, we are not only united as the Body of Christ, the Church, but we also bear public witness to our faith in the Body of Christ, the Eucharist. Every year, we receive quizzical looks from visitors to the neighbouring National Trust gardens and I cannot help but wonder whether what they see will one day mean that they too, "may give praise to your Father in heaven" (Matthew 5:16).

Not all schools will be able to celebrate Corpus Christi so long as it falls on a Sunday, but many schools celebrate other processions during term time, such as The Crowning of the Virgin Mary in May. The ancient tradition of the procession is an excellent way to physically involve pupils in Christian devotion. It is what we would now call a kinesthetic experience, bringing all the senses into play.

Godly Play at Barlborough Hall School, Sheffield

Godly Play is an innovative approach to Christian education based on scripture, involving the ancient art of storytelling and the use of symbols and active engagement. Maria Neal, the Lay Chaplain/Godly Play Practitioner at Barlborough Hall School, explains her role and how Godly Play works in her school:

As a Godly Play practitioner I lead sessions with children at Barlborough Hall School. Through a traditional method of oral storytelling speaking of the journey of the people of God, Sacramental stories, and Parables, we discuss and challenge our views surrounding identity, values and judgements. Crucially, within these discussions there is no pressure for a predesignated answer, to tick a target or learning outcome. The pupils respond in a personally meaningful way and all contributions carry equal value. I have found the frequent "out of the mouths of babes" moments that come from this to be truly awe inspiring, and have often led me to reflect on my own understanding.

For example, a discussion of the Parable of the Mustard Seed often generates very different answers. One child decided, "The sower is Jesus and the seed is his death and resurrection, the tree is heaven and the nests are the rooms that are ready for each family, the birds are the people who have died and gone to heaven." Whilst another said, "The sower is God and the seed is me, the tree is my life and the birds are all the people who are affected by my choices, the nests are the results of things I do." Each equally confident and clear in their understanding, illustrating the personal response evoked by Godly Play.

For those who are silent I have learnt to curb the urge to provoke them and instead focus on ensuring that I am anchored in the room ready for any child seeking support. I feel confident that the power of The Word will speak to that child and their deep thoughts are stirring something that must be respected as much as the processes of art or physical play. Most of my work as a Godly Play practitioner is getting out of the way. I have learnt to listen in a new way to these children's spiritual voices and curb the teacher trained response in me to assess, evaluate and record. Removing my own ego from the classroom and rethinking my role as the gatekeeper to the "answer" allows much more space for God to work and teach.

I have had the good fortune to experience a session of Godly Play led by Maria for adults. Using sand, expressive gesture and small wooden figures, she told the tale of the exile and had a room of adults mesmerised. For more information, please visit https://www.godlyplay.uk/.

Gospel values at St Joseph's Catholic and Anglican School, Wrexham

Dr Ann Casson, a senior research fellow at Canterbury Christ Church University, conducted a major research study into the spiritual development of pupils in ten Christian-ethos schools. When she visited St Joseph's Catholic and Anglican High School in Wrexham, she was shown round the school by an enthusiastic Year 8 pupil called James. Towards the end of the tour James insisted that they visited the playing fields. Ann was somewhat sceptical, wondering if this was a tactic to delay James' return to lessons, but James was determined to show his visitor that Gospel values permeated every aspect of the curriculum. He told Ann that "we are taught to play with compassion for our opponents, we care if someone falls over on the opposite side." Ann was very struck by this and on the way back from the field asked James which Gospel value was the most important for him. "Faith," he replied, "because without faith there is nothing."

This commitment to Gospel values in the school was confirmed when Ann visited lessons. She was struck by the fact that Gospel values were woven into every lesson. In one example, she observed a Year 10 English lesson about the death of Curley's wife in *Of Mice and Men*. A natural part of the critique of the scene was an exploration of the Gospel values in evidence. The pupils highlighted the compassion shown towards Curley's wife, the forgiveness for the cruel things she had done and humility in the understanding of why she did them. Gospel values were very visible in the school, displayed on classroom walls and in planners. The values were part of the everyday language of the staff and pupils and modelled in encounters in the classroom. The pupils themselves were very clear about which values mattered most to them. Justice – "it says a lot about the school because everyone gets on and it considers the world as well." Kindness – "no school is going to work properly unless everybody is kind and tolerant of each other." Tolerance – "it is needed in lessons when people don't pick things up as fast as other people."

St Joseph's in Wrexham is an example of a school where Gospel values were woven into the fabric of school life. Pupils who are educated in such a climate breathe the air of the Gospel and begin to look at the world through the eyes of Jesus Christ. It does not happen by chance of course and requires inspired leadership from the top. At St Joseph's, Maria Rimmer was the headteacher until summer 2016 and was instrumental in ensuring that the culture of the school was permeated by Gospel values. For more information on the research of Dr Ann Casson, see *Lesson in Spiritual Development: learning from Leading Christian-ethos Secondary Schools*

(London: Church House Publishing, 2017). For more background in Gospel values, see *Gospel Values for Catholic Schools: a practical guide for today* (Chawton: Redemptorist Publications, 2017).

Lectio Divina at Downside School, Somerset

Consuelo Verdugo is the leader of the Manquehue Apostolic Community from Chile currently based at Downside, a Benedictine school in Somerset. Consuelo and her community have a passion for the word of God, especially Lectio Divina, which has deep roots in the Benedictine tradition. The Manquehue Apostolic Community is a movement of lay people based in Santiago, Chile, who follow the Rule of St Benedict to different degrees, depending on their circumstances. A group has been resident at Downside for some years now and has gradually introduced the practice of Lectio Divina throughout the school, with Lectio groups led by older pupils. This has inspired a culture of "spiritual friendship" and a willingness to help each other on the spiritual journey. Consuelo explains what Lectio means to her:

The risen Christ speaks through Sacred Scripture and we encounter him, and listen to him when we do Lectio Divina. As Philip taught the eunuch in the Acts of the Apostles (Act 8:26-40), we share with others how to use the Bible in such a way as to encounter Jesus Christ personally and to accept him as the Saviour and as the Lord and King of our lives. We have learnt this from our spiritual fathers and mothers by means of tutoría – a kind of spiritual accompaniment – and it is this experience of joyful encounter that we want to share with others in small communities where we gather to do shared Lectio Divina.

This has proved to be a very powerful experience as witnessed to by some of the students of Downside:

Lectio has helped me to get closer to God deeply and spiritually, and has helped me in my daily life, knowing that he is always there for me (Brendan, sixth form).

My week is packed with commitments and in Lectio I have time to sit back and appreciate what God does in my life (Rodney, sixth form).

It has helped my faith in God to grow and to understand the Gospel better so that when I go to Sunday Mass I understand where God is coming from. I want to continue doing Lectio after school (Derek, Head Boy).

It has helped me to have a special bond with the friends I do Lectio with.
They are the first I come to when I have a problem, they are the ones that
I seek all the time. This bond we have, has been created through Lectio.
I have a stronger friendship with them than with others because we share
a very intimate thing: we share our faith (Alex, sixth form).

Lectio Divina at St Ambrose RC Primary School, Manchester

Lectio Divina or "divine reading" describes a way of reading the scriptures
whereby we gradually let go of our own agenda and open ourselves to what God
wants to say to us. Ruth Vayro, the Headteacher of St Ambrose RC primary
School in Manchester, explains how it works in her school:

At the start of each day, in every class through school, we look at Holy Scripture
in the time honoured way of Lectio (reading), Meditatio (reflecting), Oratio
(responding to) and Contemplatio (resting in the word of God). From Year 2
upwards, the children plan and prepare this delivery and by the time the children
have reached upper school Year 5 and Year 6, they are able by this practice and
repetition, to articulate very sophisticated and thoughtful expressions of the
Word of God into their own lives and everyday situations.

Children are incredibly adept at "letting go" of their own agenda as so beautifully
demonstrated in our nursery class. Perhaps, being only three years old and only
three years away from their home with Our Father, they are able to so easily move
from our real and tangible selves to a magical world of adventure and possibility.
They enjoy the novelty of using Latin. It is "fun" to say for our youngest children.
One Reception boy compared "Lectio Divina" to a spell from Harry Potter and waved
his arms around with his pencil/wand, whilst dramatically shouting "Contemplatio!"

When I asked him to explain what he meant, he whispered quietly and explained,
"It's magic because if you listen carefully enough, you can really hear the Words
of God." Lectio Divina is a natural movement towards greater simplicity, with less
and less talking and more listening. For me it is a natural choice for use with
primary children.

Prayer bag at St Louis Primary School, Frome

Tania Henry, the RE Co-ordinator at St Louis Primary School in Frome, Somerset, explains how the prayer bag works:

At St Louis Catholic Primary School, we strongly encourage our children to develop a personal relationship with God through prayer. We aim to support families in the practice of regular prayer outside of school too. Finding time for families to sit with their children in peace and unity with God is very important.

Prayer bags go home with a different child each week. Each year group has their own prayer bag which includes a rosary, a guide to praying the rosary, a cross, a book of prayers and, most importantly, a prayer diary. The prayer diary provides the opportunity for the children and parents to share their thoughts, prayers and reflections before it is passed on to the next family. The reflections and prayers, when shared with the class and class teacher, offer a wonderful glimpse into the

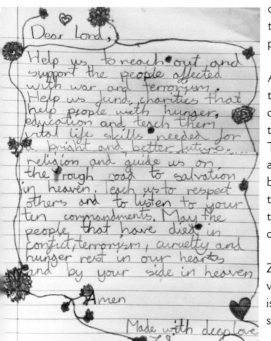

child's prayer life at home which then reciprocally supports the prayer life in school.

At St Louis, the children learn the importance of planning opportunities to listen to God so that they can hear his words. They also understand that they are God's messengers. Prayer bags enable the children to listen to and spread God's words with their families, friends and classmates.

Zofia's prayer is published here with her parents' permission. She is a Year 4 pupil and English is her second language.

School prayer at Loreto Grammar School, Altrincham

Sue Perkins, the lay chaplain at Loreto Grammar School, describes the prayer life of the school and in particular the importance of the school prayer:

Our values, sincerity, joy, freedom, truth, justice, excellence and internationalism are centred in God, rooted in Gospel values and derive from the vision of Mary Ward. All our policies and procedures are rooted in the Vision, Values and Philosophy of Education of Loreto Schools, in our own mission statement and our school prayer.

Prayer underpins all we do in school. Morning and afternoon registration and meetings begin with a prayer, either from the weekly prayer sheet distributed each week, personal petitions and prayers or in response to local and world events. Staff who aren't familiar or comfortable leading prayer are supported, girls often lead prayer too. The moments spent in silence or prayer help focus our day and are a chance to touch a space of quiet within, where we find God waiting for us. The assembly rota reflects the Church's Liturgical Year.

Weekly lunchtime Mass or services are a time of community when we come together to praise God through Word and Eucharist. Each week a different form is guided to prepare our celebration following the Liturgical Year with the readings, writing the prayers of intercession and lifting the Mass with live music. Everyone's contribution is welcomed and acknowledged. We are privileged to be supported by Father Ned and a number of other local priests. Through our retreat programme the girls have a variety of retreat experiences including the Year 10s who spend a day at the Spiritan Centre in Salford which is led by CAFOD Gappers (students on a gap year) and the Revive charity which works with refugees and people seeking asylum. These personal testimonies have a profound effect on our girls and staff.

In times of specific difficulties our community pull together and care for each other in a very profound way that is impossible to put into words. We have recently had two staff members die very suddenly, pupils who have sadly died and a number of parents and grandparents who have died. Grief is so personal and feelings, positive and negative, are acknowledged and encouraged. There are no "shoulds" in grief and each person, staff and girls, are given the space and spiritual support they need as individuals. After the Manchester Arena atrocity and London attack in June, we prayed as a community and prayers were written by girls and staff which were displayed in Chapel, a place where people came to pray privately.

Our school prayer is prayed at our whole school Masses at the start of the school year, Year 7 Welcome Mass, Christmas Mass, Easter, Year 13 leavers' Mass and our end of year Masses. It embodies who we are as a community.

O Lord our God, we dedicate this school to your glory: to the glory of the Father, source of light and life, to the glory of the Son, in whom are all the treasures of wisdom and knowledge, to the glory of the Holy Spirit, through whom the light and love of truth shine in us. May it be a place of knowledge and learning.

May all of us who work in it grow in understanding and appreciation of our world. May we grow in understanding of people above all, their dignity and powers, their weakness and needs. And that we may fulfil our task, give us courage and hope and humility and patience and a love of truth. We ask not only for learning but for wisdom.

And since there is no wisdom without love, may your Spirit of kindness and concern be in the hearts of all. Help us to disagree without bitterness, to foster ambition without envy, to give generously whatever gifts we have. In that love, may we go out to help others, to grow in understanding and freedom and love. This we ask through your Son, Jesus Christ, our Lord. Amen.

Stations of the Cross (Via Crucis) at St Gregory's Catholic College, Bath

When I was headteacher of St Gregory's Catholic College in Bath, I had the pleasure of working with the chaplain, Matthew Robinson, on the Stations of the Cross written by the pupils. We started working with a group of volunteers from all year groups in the school, pupils ranging from Year 7 to Year 10. We had a full day with them to begin with when we introduced them to the Stations of the Cross, something of the history of the devotion and some examples from art. We also showed them the passion sequence from *Jesus of Nazareth* to help them enter imaginatively into the events being described.

We then discussed what a modern set of Stations of the Cross might focus on, how might the prayers reflect the concerns of the present day through the lens of the suffering of Jesus Christ. We were very clear from the outset that we wanted to avoid a literal re-telling of the stations. It was remarkable that the pupils very quickly saw the connection between the Stations of the Cross and the "stations" of the refugees crossing Europe at that time in great numbers from Syria. To accompany the prayers, we had originally thought of using the pupils' art work or photography, but that proved to be quite challenging for younger pupils, but we did find photographs we could use for free on WikiCommons.

We also made a contact with a volunteer who had visited the refugee camp in Calais, the so-called Jungle, and allowed us to use some of his powerful photographs.

We then distributed the stations among the pupils and asked them to begin to write their own prayers and reflections, linking the Stations of the Cross to the migrant journey across Europe which was dominating the news at that time. The pupils came back with very mature and moving prayers.

Stations of the Resurrection (Via Lucis) at St Benedict's Catholic Primary School, Kent

Catholics traditionally have been more attached to the suffering of the cross than to the joy of the resurrection. The Stations of the Cross (Via Crucis) is a very ancient devotional practice, probably started in Jerusalem not many years after the events of the passion and death of Jesus. Disciples "followed" Jesus through the "stations" or main events of the passion: condemnation by Pilate, carrying of the cross and so on. In more recent times a new devotion focused on the Stations of the Resurrection, all based in scripture passages, has proved very popular. In 2001, this new devotion was commended by the Vatican's *Directory on Popular Piety and the Liturgy*. The Stations of the Resurrection can be found at https://www.catholicnewsagency.com/resources/liturgy/easter-season/via-lucis-way-of-the-light.

One headteacher, Barbara Salamonczyk, recalls how her local priest introduced the devotion to her school:

My priest, Father Bart, introduced me to "Via Lucis", the Way of Light. He had used it once in a Parish and talked me through these Stations of the Resurrection which are the Easter response to the Stations of the Cross. I adapted it for children using scripture, music, mimes performed by children from all year groups and a backdrop of a Powerpoint of beautiful art representing each Station. I divided it into two parts beginning with the first seven Stations. Each took about half an hour, which was a perfect length for this new reflection.

At the end of the service Father Bart presented each class with a mini paschal candle lit from the new parish paschal candle, taking the light of Christ to each classroom, staffroom and office. These candles were placed in the prayer corners of each room and will be used throughout the year when daily prayers are said. This was a very uplifting whole school service and really filled us with joy at the beginning of the summer term.

The Stations of the Resurrection would be an ideal way to introduce pupils to the passages of scripture which celebrate the appearances of the risen Christ. As Barbara has suggested, perhaps the fourteen stations cold be divided into two services, or spread across several weeks leading up to the final station, the descent of the Holy Spirit at Pentecost.

Wednesday Word at St Thomas More Catholic High School, Crewe

Katherine Packham, Assistant Head at St Thomas More Catholic High School in the heart of Crewe, explains the school's approach to prayer:

It is a school with many backgrounds, cultures, languages, faiths, but at the centre lies Jesus Christ. In all we do, think, speak and act we have Jesus right in the middle, buried deep but shining through. The school was built by the parishioners of Crewe and Nantwich and it continues to be at the heart of the local Catholic community. We give thanks to our parish priests and deacons for their support and love shown to St Thomas More. Prayer is integral, it is so important for reflection, quiet time, community worship, relationship building with Our Lord, tradition, soul time!

Prayer at St Thomas More comes in all shapes and sizes. Form tutors have daily collective worship, this is either in Spiritual Faith Development time – 20 minutes with form tutors every day – or in assembly – twice a week. Prayer can be led by a pupil or the tutor and can either be set prayer or private intentions shared together within the group. Pupils feel safe praying at St Thomas More and will not be shy in leading. Each Wednesday, there are no assemblies as the Spiritual Faith Development time is Wednesday Word. This is a time of reflection on the coming Sunday's Gospel reading. The reading allows the pupils to see its relevance to today's world and includes the Gospel passage, a relevant video, a discussion point and prayer. The Wednesday Word publication (no more than a side of A4) can then be taken home, which becomes another form of spiritual outreach to parents.

Pupils are immersed in prayer throughout the year at key events, Christmas, Easter and Summer liturgies, Mass during times of celebration, feast days and key school moments. Year 5s come to St Thomas More for a day's retreat, Year 7s go on retreat to the Conway centre as part of their transition to High School, Year 8s have their confirmation retreat, all years are present at the Utopia group every Tuesday lunch time, looking at key Chaplaincy issues and celebrations. All years are present at Faith In Action (FIA) every Thursday lunch time looking to right injustices at any level, all years are invited to Biscuit Club every Wednesday Lunch which takes a Biblical passage and links this to craft, prayer, action.

Mission is always a glorious end to our school year. For the last six years we have celebrated two days at the end of the year with craft, prayer, festivals, activities, which are all themed to our Gospel message of Jesus' love for all. Past themes include, equality and diversity, Christian rock festival, remembrance, vocation. Friends of the school are Brightline, a Christian band who are coming back for the third time during this year's school mission. Our colourful school displays messages of prayer through its artwork, signage, mission statement and pupil quote walls. Pupils have now designed and painted three walls in school with messages of vocation, talent, inspiration and key Christian values. There are some great messages designed on our walls by Oscar Romero, Pope Francis, Mother Teresa and our New Testament authors.

For more information on the Wednesday Word, please visit http://www.wednesdayword.org/.

Voluntary service at New Hall School, Chelmsford

Fr Lee Bennett, chaplain at New Hall School in Chelmsford, describes something of the history of the school and the background to the voluntary service programme:

New Hall School, founded in Liège in 1642, is one of England's oldest Catholic schools which, since 1799, has resided just outside Chelmsford in a beautiful parkland setting dominated by the former Beaulieu Palace, once home to King Henry VIII.

The school was established by the Canonesses of the Holy Sepulchre, no longer physically involved in the daily running of the school, but whose presence is still felt throughout. The award-winning New Hall Voluntary Service continues their legacy of outreach to the local community. It involves all students and a number of staff, who volunteer in one of the many groups offered each week, including lunch clubs for the elderly, a social club for adults with learning or physical difficulties, a gardening club and a group which helps at a local special needs school.

The Chapel, situated in the heart of the school, has been a place of daily prayer for over 200 years. It provides a sanctuary of peace and calm for all at New Hall, regardless of their personal faith. Daily Mass is offered, as well as on Holy Days of Obligation. All members of the community are valued for their unique, intrinsic worth as children of God and those of all faiths are welcomed and encouraged to recognise the value and beauty of Catholicism, and how it can illuminate our lives. A "Catholic Exploration" group is run for staff interested in learning more about the faith, and each year a number of students are baptised and welcomed into communion with the Catholic Church. In addition, a strong working relationship is maintained with the local Anglican parish. Anglican clergy form an ecumenical partnership with the Chaplaincy team in preparing Catholic and Anglican candidates for Confirmation together and regular Eucharistic services are held by the local vicar for any student or staff member who wishes to attend.

Students are encouraged to take active roles in the religious aspects of school life, serving at Mass or acting as role models for younger students as Chaplaincy Prefects or members of the "Willow" group. "Willow" is composed of Sixth Form volunteers, with each member assigned to a Year 7-9 form group to act as a mentor, role model and listening ear, especially treasured by Year 7 students as they settle into life at senior school. Within the school, the Theology Department has an outstanding reputation as one of the highest-performing academic departments. The relationship that it enjoys with the Chaplaincy is that of two distinct but complementary departments.

Questions for teachers and senior leaders to reflect on

What understanding of prayer do you want your pupils to leave you with?

Do you ask the pupils how their understanding of prayer is developing over their years with you?

What kind of daily programme would ensure that your school is a prayerful community?

How often do you monitor and review the prayer practice in the school?

How can you support or encourage adults in the community who feel distant from prayer to participate or even lead prayers in school?

How can you support or encourage your parents to engage in the prayer life of the school?

Do you have a developmental programme for the prayer life of the school for each year group, including an induction for those pupils who come to you with little experience of prayer?

Have you ever considered what kind of young people you want to develop in your school? What are the values and virtues you would like to see growing in them?

In addition to the questions above, each diocese will also have its own framework for monitoring and reviewing the prayer life of the school. This will usually be found in the diocese's Section 48 framework, or in a Church of England school, the national SIAMS framework. These frameworks often have questions to consider against criteria for assessment. The concept of monitoring and evaluating prayer may seem jarring to begin with. How can you judge something as personal as prayer, the way Ofsted judges lessons? Well, prayer is more often than not public in Catholic and Church of England schools and it is possible to neglect this aspect of the life of the school or conduct prayers with little imagination or engagement from the pupils, so it is entirely appropriate that a diocesan inspection includes a review of the prayer life of the school. When carried out with courtesy and sensitivity, an inspection of this kind should be helpful and provide useful ideas for the school to improve its practice.

Quotations to stimulate individual or group reflection

"Moved by God's Holy Spirit, we can change the face of the earth."

YOUCAT: *Youth Catechism of the Catholic Church*

"Knowledge is not to be considered as a means of material prosperity and success, but as a call to serve and to be responsible for others."

The Catholic School
(The Sacred Congregation for Catholic Education, 1977), 55

"Here is the God I want to believe in: a Father who, from the beginning of creation, has stretched out his arms in merciful blessing, never forcing himself on anyone, but always waiting, never letting his arms drop down in despair, but always hoping that his children will return so that he can speak words of love to them and let his tired arms rest on their shoulders. His only desire is to bless."

Henri Nouwen, *The Return of the Prodigal Son*
(London: Darton, Longman and Todd, 1994)

"The Catholic school loses its purpose without constant reference to the Gospel and a frequent encounter with Christ. It derives all the energy necessary for its educational work from Him and thus 'creates in the school community an atmosphere permeated with the Gospel spirit of freedom and love.' In this setting the pupil experiences his dignity as a person before he knows its definition."

The Catholic School
(The Sacred Congregation for Catholic Education, 1977), 55

"The young people we are educating today will become the leaders of the 2050s. What will religion's contribution be to educating younger generations to peace, development, fraternity in the universal human community? How are we going to educate them to faith and in faith? How will we establish the preliminary conditions to accept this gift, to educate them to gratitude, to a sense of awe, to asking themselves questions, to develop a sense of justice and consistency? How will we educate them to prayer?"

Educating Today and Tomorrow: A Renewing Passion
(Congregation for Catholic Education, 2014)

"One of the most distinctive features of the Catholic school and its ethos is the conscious fostering of prayer and sacramental life. These are not just the rituals of a community of faith, but they subtly communicate a vision of the human person as a spiritual reality with a vocation and a destiny beyond material and social aspiration."

Fr James Hanvey SJ, Visions for Leadership
(London: Heythrop Institute for Religion, Ethics and Public Life, 2009)

"The individual pursuit of happiness as defined by consumer culture still absorbs much of our time and energy. All this is true, and yet the sense that there is something more presses in. Great numbers of people feel it: in moments of reflection about their life; in moments of relaxation in nature; in moments of bereavement and loss. Our age is very far from settling into a comfortable unbelief."

Charles Taylor, A Secular Age, quoted in Doing Good: A Future for Christianity in the 21st Century
(Theos, 2016)

"Today's prosperity seems to have clipped the continent's wings and lowered its gaze. Europe has a patrimony of ideals and spiritual values unique in the world, one that deserves to be proposed once more with passion and renewed vigour, for it is the best antidote against the vacuum of values of our time, which provides a fertile terrain for every form of extremism."

Pope Francis to EU Leaders, March 2017

"The Church herself is called to learn from young people. Many saints among the youth give shining testimony to this fact and continue to be an inspiration for everyone."

Young People, the Faith and Vocational Discernment
(Preparatory Document for the XV Synod of Bishops)

"Do not be disheartened in the face of the difficulties that the educational challenge presents! Educating is not a profession but an attitude, a way of being; in order to educate it is necessary to step out of ourselves and be among young people to accompany them in the stages of their growth. Give them hope and optimism for their journey in the world. Teach them to see the beauty and goodness of creation. The sole objective of the educating community is to develop mature young people who are simple, competent and honest, who know how to live with fidelity, who can live life as a response to God's call, and their future profession as a service to society."

Pope Francis, quoted in *Educating Today and Tomorrow*
(The Congregation for Catholic Education, 2014)

"I get up half an hour early every day at 5.30 am so that I can pray and I use an online resource called Sacred Space (www.sacredspace.ie). It's been my lifeline as a headteacher. The reading this morning was all about the bread of life and it was wonderful because as a headteacher you get those days when you think 'I haven't got a clue. I wish somebody had given me a map when I started this because what on earth am I doing' and the contemplation that went with it was to the effect that God is always looking after you and nurturing you."

Secondary headteacher,
quoted in *How to Survive Working in a Catholic School*
Redemptorist Publications, 2013

"We really live outside of ourselves. There are very few humans who truly live inside themselves and this is why there are so many problems... In each person's heart, there is something like a small, intimate space, where God comes down to speak alone with that person. And this is where a person determines his or her own destiny, his or her own role in the world. If each of the people with so many problems were to enter at this moment this small space, and, once there, were to listen to the voice of the Lord which speaks in our own conscience, how much could each one of us do to improve the environment, society, the family with whom we live?"

Oscar Romero, *Through the Year with Oscar Romero: Daily Meditations*
(London: Darton, Longman and Todd, 2006)

"The aim of prayer, in fact, is to attain that point where we do the will of God, not that God should do our will. Our prayers do not change the plan of God's love for us, but it is the gifts which God grants in prayer which transform us and which bring us into harmony with his will."

Enzo Bianchi, *Why Pray, How to Pray*
(London: St. Paul's, 2014)

"Prayer is the life of Jesus coming alive in you, so it is hardly surprising if it is bound up with a certain way of being human which is about reconciliation, mercy and freely extending the welcome and the love of God to others."

Rowan Williams, *Being Christian*
(London: SPCK, 2014)

"Prayer does not change God, but it changes the person who prays."

Soren Kierkegaard, quoted in *YOUCAT: The Youth Catechism of the Catholic Church*

[1] Leeds Diocese, Guidelines on Nurturing Collective Worship in a Catholic Primary School, https://www.google.co.uk/ search?q=(7)+Leeds+Diocese%2C+Guidelines+on+Nurturing+Collective+ Worship+in+a+Catholic+Primary+School, accessed 3 October 2017.

[2] Ronald Rolheiser, *Prayer: Our Deepest Longing* (Cincinnati: Franciscan Media, 2013), 27.

[3] Ibid., 37.

[4] Ibid., 40.

[5] *The New Dictionary of Theology* (Dublin: Gill and Macmillan, 1990), 592.

[6] *Prayer*, 29.

[7] General Norms for the Liturgical Year and Calendar, 1.

[8] Pope Francis, Homily 1 November 2016 https://w2.vatican.va/content/francesco/en/homilies/2016/documents/papa-francesco_20161101_omelia-svezia-malmo.html, accessed 13 August 2017.

[9] Padraig O'Tuama, *Daily Prayer with the Corrymeela Community* (Canterbury Press, 2017), xiv.

[10] *Prayer*, 29.

Some useful websites
for further prayer resources

CAFOD
Prayer resources
http://cafod.org.uk/Pray/Prayer-resources
http://cafod.org.uk/Education/Youth-leaders-and-chaplains

CJM music
https://www.cjmmusic.com/ministry-2/

Corrymeela
http://www.corrymeela.org/

CYMFED – Detailed typology
http://cymfed.org.uk/wp-content/uploads/2013/06/CYMFed-Detailed-Typology.pdf

Daily scripture and Divine Office readings
http://universalis.com/

EducareM
http://www.educarem.org.uk/

Faith and worship
http://faithandworship.com/prayers.htm

Flame 2017
10,000 reasons to build a wall
http://cymfed.org.uk/flame2017/

Jimmy Mizen Foundation
http://forjimmy.org/

L'Arche
http://www.larche.org.uk/spirituality1

Meditation
http://christianmeditation.org.uk/

Pray as you go
https://www.pray-as-you-go.org/home/

Sacred space
https://www.sacredspace.ie/

Saint Vincent de Paul Society
https://www.svp.org.uk/involve-young-people

Salesians of Don Bosco
http://catholicyouthwork.com/

Ten Ten Theatre
http://www.tentenresources.co.uk/

The Forgiveness Project
Awareness Education Transformation
http://theforgivenessproject.com/

The Jesuit Institute UK
An Introduction to the Mass
http://jesuitinstitute.org/Resources/3%20
An%20Introduction%20to%20the%20Mass.pdf

Three-minute retreat
http://www.loyolapress.com/3-minute-retreats-daily-online-prayer

YOUCAT
YOUCAT: Youth Prayer Book
www.youcat.org